MEET THE AUTHOR

Ina C. Boyd, a graduate of the College of New Rochelle, New York, has also pursued post graduate studies at Harvard University, Boston College, and Boston University. She developed her culinary skills through studies at Madeline Kamman's "Modern Gourmet, Inc.," and Haslam's "School of Pastry and Cake Decorating."

In conjunction with the successful publication of **Cocktails and Hors d'Oeuvres,** Ina has appeared on NBC-TV's "Woman '78" and ABC-TV's "Good Day Show." She currently teaches cooking and is an active member of both "Women's Culinary Guild" and Elizabeth Schlesinger Culinary Collection at Radcliffe College. Ina is married to attorney F. Keats Boyd, Jr., and has three children, Keats, Bonnie and Chris.

YOU CAN BE ASSURED OF A PERFECT COCKTAIL HOUR EVERYTIME WITH THIS UNIQUE 2 IN 1 COCKTAIL AND HORS D'OEUVRES GUIDE

- Learn how to prepare a wide variety of popular hors d'oeuvres quickly and easily. Hot and cold hors d'oevures are presented in separate sections for ready reference.

- New tips are included for serving wine and cocktails that will be of benefit to even the expert. A wide variety of cocktail, wine and hors d'oeuvres ideas — from usual requests to the very special — are covered in detail.

- For easy reference this book is divided into two sections: Cocktails at the front, Hors d'Oeuvres at the rear.

- As with all Nitty Gritty Cookbooks, the recipes are easy to follow and are printed one per page, in large, easy-to-read type.

- For added convenience, this book is uniquely designed to take a minimum of counter space and to keep your place when pressed open.

SATISFACTION GUARANTEE—If you are not completely satisfied with any Nitty Gritty book, we will gladly refund your purchase price. Simply return it to us within 30 days along with your receipt.

**To My Family
With Love**

With special thanks to:

My husband, Keats, who has always encouraged, appreciated, and supported my endeavors;

and to my friend, Rosemary Matton, for her many hours of help in manuscript preparation;

and to all those, too numerous to mention by name, who have so thoughtfully and generously shared ideas and suggestions.

Cocktails

by
Ina C. Boyd

Illustrated by Mike Nelson

A Nitty Gritty Book*
Published by
Nitty Gritty Productions
P.O. Box 5457
Concord, California 94524

*Nitty Gritty Books—Trademark
Owned by Nitty Gritty Productions
Concord, California

ISBN 0-911954-45-7
Library of Congress Catalog Card Number: 77-93841

COCKTAILS SECTION
TABLE OF CONTENTS

See Hors d'Oeuvres Table of Contents
in middle of book.

Introduction to Cocktails

Cocktail time is one of the most pleasant ways of sharing and relaxing with family and friends. It can be a happy gathering, an intimate interlude, or simply a change in pace at the end of a busy day.

Since cocktails, along with hors d'oeuvres, set the mood of the occasion, we give it our special attention. With a little time and thought, you can add some excitement to basic drinks. Tall, cool drinks for warm days; hot drinks laced with a variety of liqueurs for those cold, chilly nights; party punches for ease at your next large gathering; and exotic drinks for elegance and fun; all are presented in this collection.

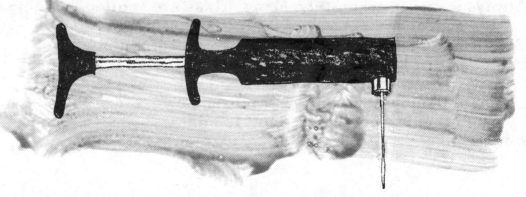

1

Tips For Making Drinks

Before anyone can be admitted to the bar, it is appropriate that he or she prepare to pass a bar examination. We therefore submit the following review course of "bar basics" to assist you.

BASIC RULES

Always use sparkling clean glassware.
Always use fresh ice.
Always serve iced drinks well chilled—the colder the better
Always measure accurately. Many drinks are spoiled by being too weak or too strong.
Superfine sugar dissolves more easily than granulated
Stir clear drinks and all-liquor drinks.
Gently stir carbonated drinks.
Shake or blend drinks with fruit juices, powdered mixes, sugar, egg, cream or other ingredients difficult to mix
Add garnishes for eye appeal

BASIC BAR EQUIPMENT

There is an almost endless list of bar accessories and gadgets available. The following are the ones we consider the most useful.

jigger with half and quarter ounces
sturdy mixing glass or pitcher
cocktail shaker
bar strainer
measuring spoons
measuring glass graded to 4 ounces
stirring rod or long spoon
muddler
corkscrew
can and bottle opener
paring knife
small cutting board
ice bucket with tongs
lemon squeezer
electric blender

3

BASIC GLASSWARE

Certainly not all of these glasses are needed. Many highballs and other long drinks are served in double old-fashioned glasses, cocktails are often served on-the-rocks in regular old-fashioned glasses, and good contemporary wine glasses can serve many needs.

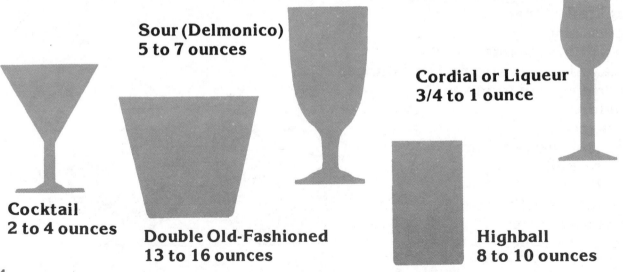

Sour (Delmonico)
5 to 7 ounces

Cordial or Liqueur
3/4 to 1 ounce

Cocktail
2 to 4 ounces

Double Old-Fashioned
13 to 16 ounces

Highball
8 to 10 ounces

Collins
10 to 14 ounces

Pilsner
10 ounces

Old-Fashioned
6 to 9 ounces

All Purpose Wine
7 to 10 ounces

Others:

Brandy Snifter — 8 to 12 ounces

Goblet — 8 to 12 ounces

Julep — 10 to 12 ounces

Mug — 9 ounces

Punch Cups — 6 ounces

Tulip Champagne — 9 ounces

5

BASIC CONTENTS OF YOUR BAR

While the size of the bottles may vary depending on your frequency of use, a basic bar should have the following:

Blended Whiskey	Vermouth, dry (French) and sweet (Italian)
Bourbon	Cocktail Sherry
Brandy	2 to 3 favorite liqueurs (see page 54)
Gin	Table Wines — white, rose and red
Light Rum	Beer
Scotch	Soft drinks and juices for non-drinking friends
Vodka	

Other Ingredients and Garnishes:
"Instant Bar Mix," page 7
Bitters
Superfine Sugar
Prepared Mixes
Mixers — club soda, tonic water, gingerale, 7-Up, collins mix, cola
Garnishes — cherries, olives, orange slices, cocktail onions

"INSTANT BAR MIX"

This mix can be prepared in advance for your convenience and is a key ingredient in a number of superb, professional drinks. It is as simple to make as instant coffee. Just add boiling water to granulated sugar. Then add pure fresh lemon juice or Minute Maid's "100% Pure Lemon Juice" found in the frozen foods section of your supermarket. Store "Instant Bar Mix" in the refrigerator. It will keep for several weeks.

2 ozs. boiling water
5 tbs. sugar
4 ozs. pure lemon juice

Pour boiling water over sugar. Stir well to completely dissolve sugar. Add lemon juice and stir well. This makes enough for about 4 drinks. You may easily double, triple, etc., the recipe so you will have a reserve on hand. It will keep for several weeks. Shake or stir well before using.

BASIC MEASUREMENTS

1 dash	4 - 8 drops	1 tenth	12.8 ounces
1 teaspoon	1/8 ounce	1 pint	16 ounces
3 teaspoons	1 tablespoon	1 fifth	25.6 ounces
1 tablespoon	1/2 ounce	1 quart	32 ounces
1 pony	1 ounce	1 liter	33.8 ounces
1 jigger	1-1/2 ounce	1 magnum	52 ounces
1 wine glass	4 ounces	1/2 gallon	64 ounces
1 split	6 ounces	1/2 lime	1/2 oz.
1 cup	8 ounces	1/2 lemon	1/2 - 3/4 oz.

BASIC QUANTITIES

1 jigger = 1-1/2 ounces

1 pint (16 ozs.)	pours 10 jiggers
1 fifth (25.6 ozs.)	pours 17 jiggers
1 quart (32 ozs.)	pours 21 jiggers
1 liter (33.8 ozs.)	pours 22 jiggers
1 half-gallon (64 ozs.)	pours 42 jiggers

BASIC ESTIMATES

The following estimates are based on 1-1/2 ounces (1 jigger) of liquor per drink, or 17 drinks per fifth (25.6 ounces). Allowing 3 drinks per person for before dinner cocktails and 4 drinks each for a party, the following chart will be helpful in estimating how many fifths you should have on hand. Keep in mind that some drinks use more than the estimated 1-1/2 ounces. To be on the safe side where the estimated amount needed comes close to using the total amount suggested, substitute quarts for fifths which will give you an additional 6 ounces or 4 jiggers per bottle.

Number of People	Number of Drinks Cocktails	Ounces	Number of Fifths to Have On Hand	Number of Drinks Party	Ounces	Number of Fifths to Have On Hand
4	12	18	1	16	24	1
6	18	27	2	24	36	2
8	24	36	2	32	48	2
10	30	45	2	40	60	3
12	36	54	3	48	72	3
20	60	90	4	80	120	5

Apertifs

Traditionally, aperitifs are aromatic wines served before dinner to stimulate appetites and set a receptive mood for the food to follow. A number of delightful predinner aperitifs have been developed which perform this function beautifully. Dubonnet is one of the most popular imports from France and is now made in the United States. It is made from sweetened red wine to which astrigency is given by adding bitter bark and quinine. There is also a white Dubonnet. Vermouth which is widely used as an ingredient in cocktails such as Martinis and Manhattans is also a very popular aperitif. A favorite with the Italians is the bitter aperitif called Campari. Mixed with soda it is quite refreshing. It is interesting that vodka had its beginnings as an aperitif. The original vodka served in Russia was very different from the vodka we know today.

AMERICANO

Campari is a colorful Italian aperitif.

3 ozs. sweet vermouth
1-1/2 ozs. (1 jigger) Campari
2 to 3 ice cubes
twist of orange or lemon peel

Combine vermouth and Campari in an old-fashioned glass with ice cubes. Twist the peel into the mixture. Garnish and stir.

CAMPARI LILLET

Another favorite aperitif is the French Lillet.

3 ozs. Lillet
2 ice cubes
1-1/2 tsp. Campari
twist of orange peel

Pour Lillet over ice cubes in a wine glass. Add Campari. Rub orange peel around the rim of the glass and drop into mixture.

LILLET ON-THE-ROCKS

4 ozs. Lillet
2 or 3 ice cubes
twist of lemon peel

Pour Lillet in a wine glass over ice. Rub a twist of lemon on the rim of the glass and drop into mixture.

DUBONNET ON-THE-ROCKS

One of the most popular aperitifs is Dubonnet. White is drier, but the sweeter red becomes more tart with a twist of lemon.

4 ozs. red or white Dubonnet
3 or 4 ice cubes
twist of lemon peel

Pour Dubonnet into an old-fashioned glass over ice cubes. Twist lemon peel over the glass and add to drink.

KIR

Creme de Cassis is a black currant syrup from Dijon, France.

6 ozs. dry white wine
1 tbs. Creme de Cassis
2 or 3 ice cubes
twist of lemon peel

In a large chilled wine glass, add ice cubes, Creme de Cassis, and dry white wine. Twist the lemon peel and drop into the glass.

KIR ROYALE — Follow the recipe for Kir using champagne in place of white wine.

14

VERMOUTH ON-THE-ROCKS

3 ozs. dry or sweet vermouth
2 or 3 ice cubes

Pour vermouth over ice cubes in an old-fashioned glass.

VERMOUTH CASSIS

4 ozs. dry vermouth
1 tbs. Creme de Cassis
2 or 3 ice cubes
2 ozs. club soda
twist of lemon peel

Mix vermouth and Creme de Cassis. Pour into highball, double old-fashioned, or large wine glass over ice cubes. Fill glass with soda and stir. Twist lemon peel over glass and drop into drink.

VERMOUTH HALF AND HALF

2 ozs. dry French vermouth
2 ozs. sweet Italian vermouth
2 or 3 ice cubes
twist of lemon peel

Pour dry vermouth and sweet vermouth in an old-fashioned glass over ice and stir. Twist lemon peel over the glass and drop into drink.

Cocktails

The first cocktail is said to have been served during the American Revolution in 1776 by Betsy Flanagan. She served Washington's officers, who frequently came to her tavern, a mixed drink of rum, rye and fruit juices. She decorated each drink with a tail feather from a prosperous Tory neighbor's rooster. As the officers cheered, a French soldier in the group toasted all with "Vive le coq's tail." We add, "Cheers to Betsy Flanagan and the Frenchman" for their delightful contribution to early America and for this fascinating tale!

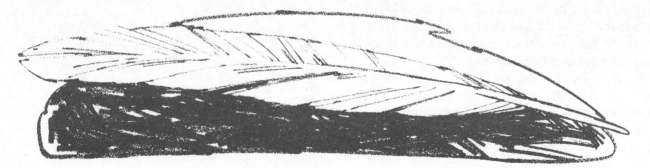

Gin

Gin was introduced into England in the 17th century by English soldiers who brought it back from Holland. It had been created as a medicine by a Dutch chemist and was sold only in apothecaries' shops. It proved so popular that many apothecaries set up distilleries of their own.

Gin is distilled from grain and flavored with juniper berries and other botanicals such as coriander. Each gin distiller carefully guards his recipe since the botanicals he uses are what gives his brand its own distinctive flavor.

Gin requires no aging but most distillers do age it. It is colorless, though some brands may be golden because of being aged in certain kinds of barrels.

TRADITIONAL MARTINI (3 to 1)

1-1/2 ozs. (1 jigger) gin
1/2 oz. dry (French) vermouth

Chill glass. Fill martini pitcher with cracked ice. Add gin, then vermouth. Stir briskly until well chilled. Strain into frosty stemmed cocktail glass or over-the-rocks in an old-fashioned glass. Garnish with an olive.

DRY MARTINI (5 to 1)

2-1/2 ozs. gin
1/2 oz. dry (French) vermouth

Mix the same as for Traditional.

EXTRA DRY MARTINI(8 to 1)

2 ozs. gin
1/4 oz. dry (French) vermouth

Mix the same as for Traditional.

GIBSON

2 ozs. gin
1/2 oz. dry (French) vermouth

Mix the same as for a traditional martini. Garnish with cocktail onion.

GIMLET

2 ozs. gin
1/2 oz. Rose's Lime Juice

Shake with ice and strain into cocktail glass, straight-up or on-the-rocks.

ORANGE BLOSSOM

1-1/2 ozs. (1 jigger) orange juice
1-1/2 ozs. (1 jigger) gin

Shake with cracked ice and strain into cocktail glass, straight-up or on-the-rocks.

PINEAPPLE-GRAPEFRUIT COOLER

2-1/2 jiggers pineapple-pink grapefruit juice
1 jigger gin
cracked ice

Measure juice and gin into a tall glass filled with ice. Stir. Serve with straws.

ORIGINAL TOM COLLINS

juice of 1 lemon
1 tsp. sugar
2 ozs. gin
club soda

Shake lemon juice, sugar and gin well. Pour into a glass. Add ice cubes. Fill glass with soda. Garnish with slices of orange and lemon and a cherry.

TOM COLLINS

2 ozs. gin
collins mix

Pour gin into a tall glass filled with ice cubes. Add collins mix. Stir gently. Add fruit slices and a cherry.

GIN RICKEY

juice of 1/2 lime
2 ozs. gin
4 ozs. club soda

Squeeze lime juice into highball glass and drop the rind in. Add ice cubes, gin and club soda. Stir gently.

GIN AND TONIC

2 ozs. gin (vodka, rum or whiskey)
tonic
quartered lime

Pour gin into a tall or old-fashioned glass with ice. Add tonic and stir gently. Squeeze lime into glass and drop rind in.

GIN FIZZ

1-1/2 ozs. "Instant Bar Mix," page 7
2 ozs. gin
club soda
cracked ice

Measure Bar Mix and gin into blender container. Blend and pour over cracked ice in a tall glass. Fill with soda. Stir lightly and add a sprig of mint.

SILVER FIZZ — Add 1 teaspoon cream to gin fizz.

RAMOS FIZZ

1-1/2 ozs. "Instant Bar Mix," page 7
2 ozs. gin
2 tbs. cream
1/4 tsp. Cointreau
1/4 tsp. orange flower water*
3 or 4 ice cubes
club soda (optional)

Measure Bar Mix, gin, cream, Cointreau, orange flower water and ice cubes into blender container. Blend until mixture is thick and frothy. Pour into a chilled glass and add club soda.

*orange flower water can be found in gourmet food stores.

SNOWBALL FIZZ

1 oz. grapefruit juice
1 oz. orange juice
2 ozs. gin
1 egg white
1 tsp. sugar
3 or 4 ice cubes

Combine ingredients in blender container. Blend and pour into a chilled cocktail or wine glass.

SINGAPORE SLING

2 ozs. gin
3/4 oz. cherry brandy
3/4 oz. lemon juice
1 tsp. sugar

Shake ingredients well with cracked ice and pour into collins glass. If desired, add a bit of soda. Garnish with pineapple and a cherry.

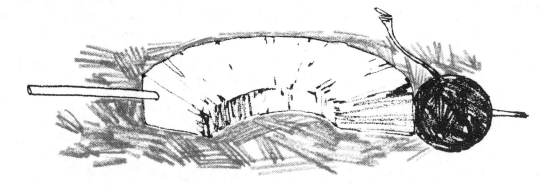

Rum

Rum is the romantic drink that brings to mind pirates and tropical breezes. It is distilled from the fermented juice of sugar cane and aged in uncharred barrels where it picks up very little color. Caramel is added to make dark rum.

There are two main kinds of rum, light-bodied and heavy-bodied. Light-bodied rums can be either light or dark in color. Dark is a bit sweeter, but light the most popular. Light-bodied rums come from Puerto Rico, Cuba and the Virgin Islands. Heavy-bodied rums are more pungent and sweeter because they are distilled by a different process which allows a fuller body to develop. They come from Jamaica, Barbados, Demerara, Martinique and Trinidad.

AUNT AGATHA

3 ozs. (2 jiggers) orange juice
1-1/2 ozs. (1 jigger) light rum
3 or 4 ice cubes
dash of bitters, optional

Pour orange juice, then rum over ice cubes in an old-fashioned glass. Add bitters and stir.

BACARDI COCKTAIL

1-1/2 ozs. (1 jigger) light Bacardi Rum
juice of 1/2 lime
1/2 tsp. grenadine

Shake ingredients with ice. Strain into cocktail glass.

CRANBERRY FROTH

5 ice cubes, cracked
1/4 cup cranberry juice
2 ozs. rum
1-1/2 ozs. "Instant Bar Mix," page 7

Blend ingredients in an electric blender. Serve in chilled glass.

CARIBE COCKTAIL

3/4 oz. "Instant Bar Mix," page 7
1 oz. pineapple juice
1-1/2 ozs. (1 jigger) light rum

Pour juice, then rum over crushed ice in an old-fashioned glass. Stir and serve.

CUBA LIBRE

juice of 1/2 lime or lemon
2 ozs. rum
Coca Cola

Pour juice over ice cubes in a tall glass. Add rum. Fill glass with cola. Drop rind in for garnish.

SOMBRERO COOLER

3 ozs. pineapple-grapefruit juice
3 ozs. light rum
sugared pineapple finger
orange slice

Pour juice and rum over ice in a double old-fashioned glass. Stir. Garnish with fruit and serve with straws.

DAIQUIRI

1-1/2 ozs. "Instant Bar Mix," page 7
2 ozs. light rum*
4 ice cubes

Blend Bar Mix, ice cubes and rum in electric blender. Pour into stemmed cocktail glass or on-the-rocks in an old-fashioned glass.

*Use dark rum if desired. Half light and half dark make a superior daiquiri.

FROZEN DAIQUIRI

Add several more ice cubes to blender with basic ingredients and blend until slushy. Serve with short straws.

FRUIT DAIQUIRIS

STRAWBERRY — Add 5 fresh or frozen strawberries to basic recipe.

PEACH — Add 1/2 fresh or canned peach or 3 ounces frozen peach to basic recipe.

BANANA — Add 1/3 ripe banana to basic recipe.

PINEAPPLE — Add 1 generous tablespoon crushed pineapple to basic recipe.

ORANGE — Add 1 ounce orange juice to basic recipe.

NECTARINE — Add 1/2 fresh nectarine to basic recipe.

PINA COLADA

The reputation of this delicious drink continues to grow. We offer two recipes—one traditional, one more exotic.

1 oz. Cream of Coconut
2 ozs. unsweetened pineapple juice
1-1/2 oz. (1 jigger) light or dark rum
crushed ice

Blend ingredients in an electric blender. Serve on-the-rocks. Add a pineapple spear for garnish.

MARY'S PINA COLADA

1 can (8 ozs.) crushed pineapple
2 tbs. coconut snow
or 1 can coconut milk
9 ozs. (6 jiggers) rum
1 tbs. superfine sugar
4 or 5 ice cubes

Blend ingredients in an electric blender. Serve on cracked ice with straws. Makes 4 servings.

RUM COLLINS — Make the same as Tom Collins, page 20, using rum in place of gin.

RUM COW

2 ozs. light rum
6 ozs. milk
1 tsp. superfine sugar
dash Angostora Bitters
dash vanilla
crushed ice
nutmeg

Blend all ingredients except nutmeg in an electric blender. Pour into a double old-fashioned glass. Dust with nutmeg.

RUM RICKEY — Make the same as Gin Rickey, page 20, using rum in place of gin.

RUM FIZZ — Make the same as Gin Fizz, page 21, using rum in place of gin.

RUM SPRITZER

1 tsp. superfine sugar
juice of 1 lime
2 ozs. light rum
club soda

Measure sugar, lime juice and rum into a large wine glass with ice cubes. Fill glass with soda. Garnish with lime.

RUM SWIZZLE

1 tsp. superfine sugar
juice of 1/2 lime
1 dash bitters
2-1/2 ozs. rum

Combine ingredients and stir vigorously with a swizzle until mixture foams. Serve over crushed ice.

MAI TAI

1/2 oz. lime juice
1/2 oz. apricot brandy
1/2 oz. Curacao
1 oz. light rum
1 oz. dark rum

Half fill a double old-fashioned glass with cracked ice. Add ingredients in the order listed. Stir gently and garnish with a pineapple stick, marachino cherry and a lime wedge. Serve with straws.

HAWAIIAN NECTAR

1/2 oz. "Instant Bar Mix," page 7
3/4 oz. pineapple-grapefruit juice
1-1/2 ozs. (1 jigger) light or dark rum

Fill an old-fashioned glass with cracked ice. Add ingredients and stir. Garnish with a finger of pineapple.

POLYNESIAN PARADISE

1 tsp. superfine sugar
1/2 oz. lime juice
3/4 oz. lemon juice concentrate
2 ozs. orange juice
1/2 oz. Curacao
2 ozs. light rum

Fill a double old-fashioned glass with cracked ice. Add ingredients and stir.

FOG CUTTER

1 oz. orange juice
2 ozs. "Instant Bar Mix," page 7
1/2 oz. gin
1 oz. brandy
2 ozs. light rum
1 tsp. Madeira wine

Fill a double old-fashioned glass with cracked ice. Pour all ingredients except Madeira over ice and stir. Float Madeira on top.

SCORPION

This is an alchemists delight. Refreshing and pleasing, it does have a sting!

4 ozs. orange juice
4 ozs. white wine
3 ozs. "Instant Bar Mix," page 7
3 ozs. rum
1/2 ozs. brandy
1/2 ozs. gin

Measure ingredients into a pitcher. Stir and serve over cracked ice in a very tall glass with straws. Makes 2 servings.

SOUTH SEAS PUNCH

1-1/2 ozs. (1 jigger) orange juice
3/4 oz. "Instant Bar Mix," page 7
juice of 1/2 lime
1/2 oz. Cointreau
2 ozs. light rum
2 or 3 ice cubes
pineapple cube and a cherry

Blend orange juice, lemon juice, lime juice, Cointreau, rum, and ice cubes together in an electric blender. Pour into a tall glass with cracked ice. Garnish with pineapple and cherry on a toothpick and the lime shell. Serve with straws.

PLANTERS PUNCH

1-1/2 ozs. "Instant Bar Mix," page 7
1/2 oz. lime juice
2 ozs. dark rum
1 oz. light rum
5 ice cubes

Blend ingredients in an electric blender. Pour into a tall glass with cracked ice. Garnish with a cherry, lemon or lime slice, 1/2 slice orange and a sprig of mint. Serve with a straw.

TROPICAL DELIGHT

3/4 oz. "Instant Bar Mix," page 7
1 oz. orange juice
3/4 oz. light rum
1/4 oz. dark rum
1/4 oz. brandy
pineapple cube and a cherry
sprig of mint

Fill old-fashioned glass with cracked ice. Add lemon juice, orange juice, rum and brandy. Garnish with the fruit on a toothpick and a sprig of mint.

ZOMBIE

1 oz. unsweetend pineapple juice
juice of 1 lime
juice of small orange
1 tsp. powdered sugar
1/2 oz. apricot brandy
2-1/2 ozs. light or dark rum
1 oz. Jamaica rum
1/2 cup crushed ice
pineapple spear, green and red cherry
1/2 oz. 151 proof rum
fresh mint

Blend juices, sugar, brandy, rums (not 151 proof) and ice in electric blender on low speed. Strain into frosted zombie glass. Decorate with fruit. Float 151 proof rum on top of drink. Add mint and serve with a straw.

Tequila

Tequila is a fiery Mexican liquor distilled from the juice of a special plant that grows only in the Mexican state of Jalisco. Conditioned Mexican palates take tequila straight but more delicate Northerners prefer tequila in the form of a Margarita or Tequila Sunrise.

There is a ritual which goes with the drinking of straight tequila. A sprinkle of salt is placed on the back of one hand while thumb and forefinger of the same hand hold a slice of lime. A shot glass of tequila is held in the other hand. First you lick the salt, then the tequila is quickly swallowed, followed immediately by biting into the slice of lime. It does take a little getting used to!

MARGARITA

1 oz. fresh lime or lemon juice.
1-1/2 ozs. (1 jigger) Tequila
1 oz. Cointreau
cracked ice

Moisten cocktail glass rim with lime or lemon juice. Dip rim in salt. Shake ingredients with cracked ice. Strain into glass.

SANGRITA

3 ozs. tomato juice
juice of 1/2 lemon
juice of 1/2 orange
dash Worcestershire Sauce
4 drops Tabasco
1-1/2 ozs. (1 jigger) tequila
salt and pepper
4 ice cubes
lime wedge

Blend tomato juice, lemon and orange juice, Worcestershire and Tabasco together. Measure tequila into a tall glass with the ice cubes. Fill glass with juice mixture. Add salt and pepper. Garnish with lime wedge.

TEQUILA SUNRISE

1-1/2 ozs. (1 jigger) tequila
3 ozs. (2 jiggers) orange juice
ice cubes
1/2 oz. grenadine

Stir tequila and orange juice with ice. Strain into highball glass. Add ice cubes. Pour in grenadine slowly and allow to settle. Serve. Garnish as desired with orange slice, lime wedge, cherry and/or fresh mint.

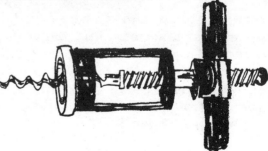

Vodka

Vodka, the most versatile of all alcoholic beverages has become extremely popular in recent years. It is highly refined and filtered, has little taste or smell and does not require aging. Vodka was originally made in Russia from potatoes, but now it is distilled from grains, primarily corn and wheat. The differences between various brands result from the variety of grains and the distilling and filtering process used. Unlike American, English and German vodka which is almost tasteless, Russian vodka is flavored with pungent herbs, nuts and berries, and Polish vodka is flavored with wild buffalo grass. These vodkas are always taken straight and ice-cold, in one swallow, along with food.

BLOODY MARY

4 drops Tabasco
3 dashes Worcestershire
1-1/2 ozs. "Instant Bar Mix," page 7
1/4 tsp. salt
1/2 tsp. pepper
1 can (12 ozs.) V-8 juice
4-1/2 ozs. (3 jiggers) vodka
celery sticks

Combine all ingredients except celery in a mixing pitcher. Stir to mix. Serve in a double old-fashioned glass filled with crushed ice. Garnish with celery stick. Makes two servings.

BULL SHOT

1 can (10-3/4 ozs.) beef bouillon
5-1/2 ozs. vodka
2 tbs. lime juice
1 can (16 ozs.) V-8 juice
dash Worcestershire
dash Tabasco
celery sticks
lime wedges

Combine first six ingredients in mixing pitcher. Serve in double old-fashioned glasses filled with cracked ice. Garnish with celery sticks and lime wedges. Makes 4 servings.

CAPE CODDER

1-1/2 ozs. (1 jigger) vodka
cranberry juice cocktail

Fill and old-fashioned glass with crushed ice. Add vodka and fill glass with cranberry juice.

CAPE COD COOLER

1-1/2 ozs. (1 jigger) vodka
1-1/2 ozs. (1 jigger) cran-grape juice
club soda
juice of 1/2 lime

Fill a double old-fashioned glass with ice. Add vodka and cran-grape juice. Fill glass with club soda. Squeeze lime into mixture and drop rind into glass.

GRAPE SHOT

1-1/2 ozs. (1 jigger) vodka
2 ozs. Seven-Up or gingerale
grape juice

Fill a double old-fashioned glass with ice. Add vodka, Seven-Up and grape juice. Stir.

HARVEY WALLBANGER

6 ozs. orange juice
1 ozs. vodka
1/2 oz. Galliano

Fill a tall glass with ice cubes. Add orange juice and vodka. Stir and splash in Galliano.

MADRAS

1-1/2 ozs. (1 jigger) orange juice
3 ozs. (2 jiggers) cranberry juice
1-1/2 ozs. (1 jigger) vodka

Measure orange juice, cranberry juice and vodka into a double old-fashioned glass filled with ice. Stir.

LEMONADE COOLER

1-1/2 ozs. (1 jigger) vodka
lemonade

Add vodka and lemonade to a tall glass filled with ice. Stir and serve with a straw.

SALTY DOG

cut lemon
salt
2 or 3 ice cubes
3 ozs. grapefruit juice
1-1/2 ozs. (1 jigger) vodka

Rub the lemon around the rim of an old-fashioned or wine glass. Dip the rim in salt. Add ice cubes, grapefruit juice and vodka to glass. Stir.

VODKA COLLINS — Mix the same as Tom Collins, page 20, using vodka.

VODKA MARTINI — Mix the same as Gin Martini, page 18, using vodka.

SCREWDRIVER

1-1/2 ozs. (1 jigger) vodka
orange juice
pineapple finger

Fill an old-fashioned or wine glass with ice cubes. Add vodka and fill glass with orange juice. Stir and garnish with pineapple finger.

VODKA ZEST

3 ozs. grapefruit juice
1-1/2 ozs. (1 jigger) vodka
1 tbs. Cointreau
lemon peel twist

Add juice, vodka and Cointreau to an old-fashioned glass filled with ice. Stir and garnish with lemon twist.

Whiskies

Whiskies are distilled from fermented mash of grain, usually corn, rye, barley or wheat, and then aged in oak barrels. When first placed in the barrels whiskey is colorless. It is during the aging process that it obtains its amber color, flavor and aroma.

The major whiskey producing countries are the United States, Canada, Scotland and Ireland. Special grains, recipes and distillation processes make the whiskey of each country distinctive.

Straight whiskey is not blended with neutral spirits or any other whiskey. Four major straights are bourbon, rye, corn and bottled-in-bond whiskey.

Blended whiskey is a blend of one or more straight whiskeys and neutral spirits.

HIGHBALL

1-1/2 to 2 ozs. whiskey
3 or 4 ice cubes
water, club soda or gingerale

Fill highball or double old-fashioned glass with ice cubes. Add whiskey, and water, club soda or gingerale. Stir.

ON-THE-ROCKS

1-1/2 to 2 ozs. Scotch, blended whiskey
    or bourbon
ice cubes
twist of lemon peel

Pour whiskey over ice in an old-fashioned glass. Add a twist of lemon peel.

MIST

1-1/2 to 2 ozs. Scotch, blended whiskey
    or bourbon
finely shaved or crushed ice
twist of lemon peel

Pour whiskey over crushed ice in an old-fashioned glass. Add twist of lemon peel. Can be served with short straws.

WHISKEY SOUR

2 ozs. Scotch, blended whiskey
    or bourbon
1-1/2 ozs. "Instant Bar Mix," page 7
4 ice cubes
orange slice and maraschino cherry

Blend liquor, Bar Mix and ice in an electric blender. Pour into a sour glass. Garnish with an orange slice and cherry.

MANHATTAN

1/2 oz. sweet (Italian) vermouth
1 dash bitters optional
1-1/2 ozs. (1 jigger) blended whiskey

Stir with ice and strain into cocktail glass. Add maraschino cherry.

DRY MANHATTAN — Use dry (French) vermouth in place of sweet. Add an olive.

PERFECT MANHATTAN

1/2 oz. dry (French) vermouth
1/2 oz. sweet (Italian) vermouth
2 ozs. blended whiskey

Stir with ice and strain into a cocktail glass. Add a cherry.

ROB ROY

1-1/2 ozs. (1 jigger) Scotch
3/4 oz. sweet (Italian) vermouth
1 dash bitters, optional

Stir ingredients with ice and strain into cocktail glass. Add lemon twist.

DRY ROB ROY — Use dry (French) vermouth in place of sweet. Add an olive.

SCARLET O'HARA

1-1/2 ozs. (1 jigger) Southern Comfort
1-1/1ozs. (1 jigger) cranberry juice
juice of 1/2 lime

Shake ingredients with crushed ice. Strain into cocktail glass.

OLD-FASHIONED

Another Kentucky contribution to the cocktail circuit is the Old-Fashioned. Along with the traditional one, we offer some variations.

1/2 lump of sugar
2 dashes of bitters
1 tsp. water or club soda
1-1/2 ozs. (1 jigger) blended whiskey

In an old fashioned glass muddle sugar, bitters and water thoroughly to dissolve sugar. Add ice cubes and whiskey. Stir and garnish with an orange slice and a cherry.

OLD-FASHIONED II

1 oz. gingerale
1 oz. orange juice
dash of cherry juice
1-1/2 ozs. (1 jigger) blended whiskey
3 ice cubes
fruit garnish

Pour ingredients into an old-fashioned glass and stir. Garnish with a slice of an orange and a cherry.

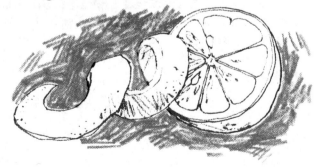

OLD-FASHIONED III

Wonderful time-savers are the cocktail garnishes preserved in syrup.

1/4 tsp. syrup from cocktail orange slices
3/4 oz. (1/2 jigger) club soda
3 ice cubes
2 ozs. bourbon
1 dash bitters
1 cocktail orange slice

Put syrup in the bottom of an old-fashioned glass. Add club soda and stir. Add ice cubes, bourbon and bitters. Stir again. Garnish with orange.

JOHN COLLINS — Make the same as Tom Collins, page 20, using whiskey in place of gin.

MINT JULEP

The Mint Julep is a tradition of the Kentucky Derby. It is important for this drink to be served in frosted glasses or silver tumblers. This can be accomplished by placing them in the freezer wet for a short time. Whether you choose glass or silver, beware of frostbite!

3 or 4 sprigs of fresh mint
1 tsp. sugar
or 1/2 oz. Cointreau
cracked ice
2 ozs. bourbon

Crush mint in 12 ounce collins or julep glass. Add sugar or Cointreau. Fill glass with cracked ice. Add bourbon. Stir until well-chilled. Decorate with more sprigs of fresh mint.

WHISKEY SOUR FREEZE

This drink is ideal for a hot summer day.

1 can (12 ozs.) frozen orange juice
1 can (6 ozs.) frozen lemonade
1 can (12 ozs.) water
1 can (12 ozs.) blended whiskey
    or bourbon
gingerale or Seven-up

Blend orange juice, lemonade, water and whiskey in electric blender. Pour into a container and freeze. To serve, spoon some of the frozen mixture into an old-fashioned glass. Add a generous splash of gingerale. Let sit a minute until gingerale seeps through the frozen mixture. Makes enough for several drinks.

Champagne and Wine Drinks

Champagne, the most elegant of all wines, makes any occasion a celebration. You can drink it at any time of day, with any course of a meal, and it is unexcelled as an aperitif.

Champagne must be served chilled but not overly so, and it should be opened with care. If the cork is allowed to fly out, too much wine and sparkle will be wasted. A better way is to slant the bottle about 45°, with a napkin placed between your hand and the neck of the bottle. Holding the cork in the other hand, slowly twist the bottle away from the cork. There will be a gentle pop but the champagne will not foam up out of the bottle.

The glass in which champagne is served is important to its enjoyment since it is desirable to retain the bubbles as long as possible. A tulip shaped glass is best and one with a hollow stem is perfect. The glass should be chilled and never filled more than half.

Still wines—white, rosé and red—make refreshing drinks and wonderful punches. They adapt well to combinations of fruits and fruit juices.

CHAMPAGNE COCKTAIL

1 small sugar cube
1 drop Angostura bitters
iced champagne
1 twist lemon peel

Place sugar in a tulip-shaped champagne glass. Drop bitters onto sugar cube. Fill glass with champagne. Add twist.

CHAMPAGNE A L'ORANGE

12 ozs. chilled champagne
12 ozs. chilled Seven-Up or gingerale
8 ozs. chilled orange juice

Combine ingredients and serve in tall wine glasses with two ice cubes in each. Garnish with an orange slice or strawberry. Makes 4 drinks.

CHAMPAGNE AND RASPBERRY SPARKLE

1 pkg. (10 ozs.) frozen raspberries
1 bottle ("fifth") champagne
1 tbs. lemon juice

Puree raspberries in blender and strain. Add lemon juice and chill well in the refrigerator. At serving time, stir to blend and add 2 to 3 tablespoons of raspberry puree to each glass. Fill glasses with champagne. Stir gently. Makes 4 drinks.

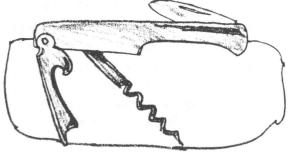

FRENCH "75"

This is especially delicious on a hot summer evening! The secret of making a superb "French 75" is using plenty of ice in the blending stage.

1-1/2 ozs. "Instant Bar Mix," page 7
2 ozs. gin
6 ice cubes
3 ozs. (2 jiggers) chilled champagne

Measure Bar Mix, gin and 4 ice cubes into blender container. Blend and pour into a chilled wine goblet. Add champagne and 2 cracked ice cubes.

FRENCH "125" — Prepare the same as French "75," using brandy in place of gin.

CRANBERRY PINEAPPLE COOLER

5 ozs. rosé wine
2 ozs. cranberry juice
2 ozs. undiluted frozen pineapple juice
3 or 4 ice cubes

In blender combine rosé wine, cranberry juice and undiluted pineapple juice. Add ice to a tall glass or double old-fashioned glass and pour in mixture.

ROSE FRAPPE

1 bottle (4/5 quart) rosé wine
1 can (6 ozs.) frozen lemonade
3/4 cup Seven-Up or gingerale

Stir together wine, lemonade and Seven-Up. Pour over ice in wine goblets.

49

SANGRIA

1 bottle red burgundy
2 squeezed oranges
1 sliced orange
1 squeezed lime
1 sliced lime
3 peaches, peeled and cut up
2 ozs. Cognac
2 ozs. Cointreau
sugar to taste
ice
strawberries

In a pitcher combine all ingredients except strawberries. Chill in refrigerator a couple of hours before serving to blend flavor. Add strawberries just before serving. Pour into large wine glasses with ice cubes. Makes 3 to 4 servings.

WHITE SANGRIA

1 bottle Chablis, chilled
1 split (6 ozs.) champagne, chilled
1 sliced lemon, slightly squeezed
ice cubes
strawberries

Combine Chablis, champagne, lemon and ice cubes. Pour into large wine glasses filled with ice. Garnish with a strawberry.

WINE COOLER

3 ozs. your favorite wine
3 ozs. collins mixer or Seven-Up

Measure wine and collins mixer into a double old-fashioned or large wine glass filled with ice. Stir and serve.

WINE SPRITZER

3 ozs. dry white or rosé wine
3 ozs. club soda
plenty of ice
a lemon quarter

Measure wine and club soda into a collins, double old-fashioned or large wine glass filled with ice. Stir. Squeeze in lemon and drop rind into glass.

WINE AND TONIC

Light and refreshing this is pleasant on a hot day.

3 ozs. white wine
3 ozs. quinine water
plenty of ice

Mix wine and quinine water in a tall glass, double old-fashioned or wine glass filled with ice. Stir well. Delicious!

After Dinner Drinks

After dinner cordials or liqueurs originated as effective medicinal or digestive aids. The word "cordial" comes from the Latin word "cor" meaning "heart" because it was thought of as a heart stimulant. Their origins date back to the 1500's. Monasteries played an important role in their development. Recipes for some have been secretly guarded for centuries. Liqueurs today are the basis for many fine cocktails as well as after dinner drinks. They are ideal for adding just the right touch to gourmet cooking.

FAVORITE LIQUEURS

These can be served in a cordial glass or over cracked ice in a cocktail glass, or mixed two parts liqueur to one part cream and served on the rocks in an old-fashioned glass.

Amaretto – a blend of almond and apricot.
Anisette – a subtle taste of licorice.
B and B – equal parts Benedictine and brandy.
Benedictine – a Cognac based liqueur with aromatic herbs.
Cointreau – orange-flavored.
Creme de Cacao – chocolate flavored
Creme de Menthe – peppermint flavored.
Curacao – orange-flavored.
Drambuie – liqueur made from Scotch.
Galliano – licorice flavored.
Grand Marnier – orange flavored Cognac brandy.
Kahlua – coffee flavored.
Triple Sec – orange flavored.

FAVORITE BRANDIES

Cognac is the unchallenged, finest brandy in the world. It is produced from grapes grown only in the Cognac region of France. Aging in oak casks and experienced tasters also contribute to the excellent quality of Cognac.

Fruit brandies are made from fruit and are aged in glass-lined casks rather than wood.

Kirsch – black cherry brandy.
Calvados – apple brandy
Framboise – raspberry brandy.

Brandies flavored with fruit
Apricot-flavored brandy.
Blackberry-flavored brandy.
Cherry-flavored brandy.
Peach-flavored brandy.

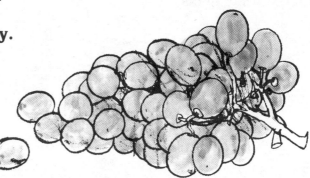

ALEXANDER

1 oz. brandy
1 oz. Creme de Cacao
1 oz. cream
3 to 4 ice cubes

Shake ingredients vigorously. Strain into a cocktail glass or on-the-rocks in an old-fashioned glass.

ALEXANDER II

1 oz. gin
1 oz. Creme de Cacao
1 oz. cream
3 to 4 ice cubes

Shake ingredients vigorously in cocktail shaker or use a blender. Strain into a cocktail glass or on-the-rocks in an old-fashioned glass.

ALEJANDRA — Same as Alexander but using Kahlua instead of Creme de Cacao.

AMARETTO

1 oz. Amaretto
1 oz. vodka
1 oz. cream
3 to 4 ice cubes

Shake ingredients vigorously in cocktail shaker. Strain into a champagne glass, or on-the-rocks in an old-fashioned glass.

BLACK RUSSIAN

2 ozs. vodka
1 oz. Kahlua
3 to 4 ice cubes

Pour vodka and Kahlua over ice in an old-fashioned glass and stir.

BRAZILIAN ICED COFFEE

1-1/2 ozs. (1 jigger) rum
1/2 cup strong coffee
1 tsp. sugar
1 oz. cream
ice cubes

Shake ingredients vigorously in a cocktail shaker or use a blender. Serve over ice in a double old-fashioned glass.

CREME DE MENTHE FRAPPE

Fill a cocktail glass with crushed ice. Add green Creme de Menthe. Serve with straws.

FRENCH CONNECTION

1-1/2 ozs. (1 jigger) brandy
3/4 oz. Amaretto
3 to 4 ice cubes

Pour brandy and Amaretto over ice cubes in an old-fashioned glass. Stir and serve.

GODFATHER

3/4 oz. Amaretto
1-1/2 ozs. (1 jigger) Scotch
3 to 4 ice cubes.

Pour Amaretto and Scotch over ice cubes in an old-fashioned glass. Stir and serve.

GOLDEN CADILLAC

1 oz. Galliano
2 ozs. white Creme de Cacao
1 oz. cream
3 to 4 ice cubes

Shake ingredients vigorously in cocktail shaker or use a blender. Pour into a cocktail glass, or serve on-the-rocks in an old-fashioned glass.

GODMOTHER

3/4 oz. Amaretto
1-1/2 ozs. (1 jigger) vodka
3 to 4 ice cubes

Pour Amaretto and vodka over ice cubes in an old-fashioned glass. Stir and serve.

GRASSHOPPER

1 oz. white Creme de Cacao
1 oz. green Creme de Menthe
1 oz. cream
3 to 4 ice cubes

Shake ingredients vigorously in cocktail shaker or use a blender. Serve in cocktail glass or champagne saucer.

HARVEY'S BRISTOL CREAM

Sip from a sherry glass or pour over ice in an old- fashioned glass. Garnish with a wedge of lime.

ITALIAN MOUSSE

1-1/4 ozs. Chocolate Mint Liqueur
1 oz. vodka
1/2 oz. cream
3 or 4 ice cubes

Shake ingredients vigorously in cocktail shaker or use a blender. Serve in a cocktail glass, champagne saucer or old-fashioned glass.

PINK SQUIRREL

1 oz. white Creme de Cacao
1 oz. Creme de Almond
3/4 oz. cream
3 to 4 ice cubes

Shake ingredients vigorously in cocktail shaker or blend in blender. Serve in a cocktail glass, or on-the-rocks in an old-fashioned glass.

RUSTY NAIL

1-1/2 ozs. (1 jigger) Drambuie
1-1/2 ozs. (1 jigger) Scotch
2 to 3 ice cubes

Pour Drambuie and Scotch over ice cubes in an old-fashioned glass. Stir and serve.

SICILIAN KISS

1 oz. Southern Comfort
1/2 oz. Amaretto

Pour ingredients over cracked ice in cocktail glass. Stir and serve.

SIDE CAR

This may also be served as a cocktail

1 oz. brandy
1 oz. Cointreau
1 oz. lemon juice
3 to 4 ice cubes

Shake ingredients vigorously in a cocktail shaker or use a blender. Serve on-the-rocks in an old-fashioned glass.

SOMBRERO

2 ozs. coffee brandy or Kahlua
2 ozs, cream
3 to 4 ice cubes

Pour brandy or Kahlua and cream over ice cubes in old-fashioned glass. Stir and serve.

STINGER

This can also be served as a cocktail.

1-1/2 ozs. (1 jigger) brandy
3/4 oz. white Cream de Menthe
ice

Mix in blender or cocktail shaker with ice. Strain into cocktail glass, or on-the-rocks in an old-fashioned glass.

VELVET HAMMER

1 oz. brandy
1/4 oz. banana liqueur
1/4 oz. Cointreau
1-1/2 ozs. cream

Shake ingredients vigorously in cocktail shaker or use a blender. Serve in an old-fashioned glass with straws.

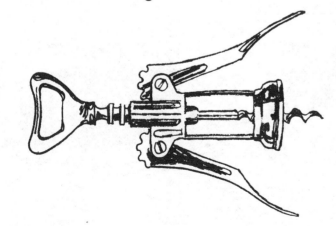

WHITE RUSSIAN

1 oz. vodka
1 oz. white Creme de Cacao
1 oz. cream
3 to 4 ice cubes

Shake ingredients vigorously in a cocktail shaker or use a blender. Strain into a cocktail glass, or pour on-the-rocks in an old-fashioned glass.

WHITE SPIDER

2 ozs. vodka
1 oz. white Creme de Menthe*
2 to 3 ice cubes

Stir vodka, Creme de Menthe and ice together until mixed. Strain into chilled cocktail glass.

*Green Creme de Menthe can be substituted for white.

Hot Drinks

Nothing takes the chill out of a winter day like a hot drink laced with spirits. If winter sports are your first love this section is made to order for you. Rum, brandy, whiskey and liqueurs blend with coffee, hot chocolate and other mixtures to make delicious concoctions guaranteed to warm you right down to your toes. What more could a skier or ice skater ask?

Hot drinks can be served in mugs, stemmed glasses or glasses with handles. If you are using a glass it's a good idea to put a spoon in the glass, round side up, and pour the hot liquid onto the spoon. This helps to distribute the heat evenly and prevents the glass from breaking.

Whatever the weather, add glamour to your next party by serving Spanish Coffee or one of its variations. It's sensational. Or, try Hot Chocolate Mint, Mocha Brandy, Tom and Jerry or Hot Buttered Rum. They're all sure to please.

BLACK BART

1 cup milk
3 heaping tsp. Nestle Quick
1 oz. light rum
1 tbs. Grand Marnier
whipped cream

Heat milk and add Quick. In a mug, long-stemmed or handled glassware, combine rum, Grand Marnier and hot chocolate. Top with whipped cream.

HOT CHOCOLATE MINT

1 cup milk
3 heaping tsp. Nestle Quick
1-1/2 ozs. Chocolate Mint Liqueur
whipped cream

Heat milk and add Quick. In a mug, long-stemmed or handled glassware, combine Chocolate Mint Liqueur and hot chocolate. Top with whipped cream.

MOCHA BRANDY

1 cup milk
3 heaping tsp. Nestle Quick
1/4 cup strong coffee
1-1/2 ozs. (1 jigger) brandy
sugar
whipped cream

Heat milk and add Quick. Combine coffee, hot chocolate and brandy. Stir in desired sugar and top with whipped cream.

GROG

1 lemon slice
2 whole cloves
1 tsp. superfine sugar
1-in. piece cinnamon stick
3 ozs. Jamaica rum
4 oz. boiling water

Stud lemon slice with cloves. Rinse an 8-ounce hot drink glass or mug with hot water. Place sugar, cinnamon stick and lemon slice in warm glass. Add rum and stir. Leave spoon in glass and add boiling water. Stir and serve.

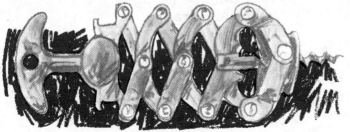

SPANISH COFFEE

Add glamour to your next party by demonstrating this masterpiece. You may also prepare ahead and serve—it still has tremendous eye appeal to say nothing about how good it tastes. This is a favorite of ours.

1 lemon wedge
long-stemmed or handled glassware
1 generous tbs. brandy
1-1/2 ozs. (1 jigger) Kahlua
sugar
freshly brewed coffee
whipped cream

Rub lemon around the rim of glass, then dip into a dish filled with sugar. In front of an alcohol burner or sterno, rotate the glass over the flame to carmelize sugar. (If preparing ahead of time, you can prepare to this point.) Place spoon in glass to prevent cracking. Warm brandy in a pan or chafing dish. Pour into glass and ignite. Then add the jigger of Kahlua and ignite. Pour in hot coffee leaving about 1-1/2 inches. Add whipped cream level with the top of the glass. Serve on a dessert plate with a spoon.

DUTCH COFFEE — Same procedure as Spanish Coffee substituting 1-1/2 ounces (1 jigger) Vandermint for Kahlua and brandy.

FRENCH COFFEE — Same procedure as Spanish Coffee substituting 1-1/2 ounces (1 jigger) Grand Marnier for Kahlua and brandy.

IRISH COFFEE — This drink was made popular at Buena Vista Cafe at Fisherman's Wharf in San Francisco. Follow same procedure as Spanish Coffee substituting 1-1/2 ounces (1 jigger) Irish Whiskey for Kahlua and brandy.

ISRAELI COFFEE — Same procedure as Spanish coffee substituting 1-1/2 ounces (1 jigger) Sabra for Kahlua and brandy.

ITALIAN COFFEE — Same procedure as Spanish Coffee substituting 1-1/2 ounces (1 jigger) Amaretto for Kahlua and Brandy.

JAMAICAN COFFEE — Same procedure as Spanish Coffee substituting 1-1/2 ounces (1 jigger) rum for Kahlua.

ROMAN COFFEE — Same procedure as Spanish Coffee substituting 1-1/2 ounces (1 jigger) Galliano for Kahlua.

CAFE ROYALE — Same procedure as Spanish Coffee substituting 1-1/2 ounces (1 jigger) brandy for Kahlua and brandy.

CAFE BRULOT

7 sugar cubes
8 ozs. (6 jiggers) brandy
1 lemon twist
2 orange twists
2 cinnamon sticks
10 whole cloves
4 cups strong, hot coffee

Place all ingredients except coffee in a chafing dish. Heat gently, stirring constantly until well warmed. Ignite and let burn about 1 minute. Slowly pour in coffee. Ladle coffee into demi-tasse cups being careful not to get any of the spices. Makes 6 to 8 servings.

CAFE DIABLE

2 tbs. sugar
5 ozs. dark rum or brandy
2 orange twists
10 whole cloves
2 1-inch cinnamon sticks
5 cups strong, hot coffee

Place all ingredients except coffee in a chafing dish. Heat gently, stirring constantly. Ignite and let burn one minute. Slowly add coffee. Ladle into cups. Makes 4 to 6 servings.

HOT BUTTERED RUM

1 lb. brown sugar
1 lb. powdered sugar
1 lb. butter
1 qt. vanilla ice cream
1 tsp. cinnamon
1 tsp. nutmeg
rum
boiling water

Heat brown sugar, powdered sugar, butter, ice cream, cinnamon and nutmeg slowly until it's like cake batter. Place in freezer until frozen. To serve, place 1 heaping tablespoon of batter in each mug. Add 2 ounces rum. Fill mug with boiling water and stir. Sprinkle with nutmeg and serve. Makes about 50 drinks.

TOM AND JERRY

12 eggs, separated
1/4 tsp. cream of tartar
3 lbs. powdered sugar
1 tsp. cinnamon
1/2 tsp. nutmeg
1 tsp. allspice
1 tsp. vanilla
rum and brandy
boiling water

Beat egg whites with cream of tartar until stiff. Beat yolks with sugar, spices and vanilla. Fold egg whites into yolk mixture. (This batter will keep for about six hours.) To serve, place 1 heaping tablespoon of batter in mug. Add 3/4 ounce each of rum and brandy. Fill mug with boiling water. Stir and sprinkle with nutmeg. Makes 48 drinks.

Punches

Party punches add a gala touch to a party. They can be prepared in advance except for adding carbonated mixes and sparkling wines, which should be well-chilled and added just before serving. Garnishes of fruit frozen in ring molds, wreaths of greens of flowers or floating fruit slices, berries or flowers, all contribute to a festive touch. Be creative!

If you don't have a punch bowl, don't let that stop you. A large pitcher or a scalloped watermelon shell can always be used. For a truly spectacular container, make a punch bowl out of a piece of ice. To accomplish this, start with a 15-inch block of ice. Let it stand at room temperature about 20 minutes. Fill a stainless steel bowl or pan which is about 8 inches in diameter with boiling water. Press this into the center of ice. Keep the bowl filled with very hot water until the well or depression is 6 inches deep. Wrap the base of the ice "bowl" in heavy duty foil and keep in freezer. This can be all prepared days in advance. Plan ahead as it does take time. When ready to serve set ice "bowl" on a tray or shallow pan to take care of melting. Wreathe base with flowers or greens to conceal pan.

BLOODY MARY PUNCH

3 qts. chilled tomato or V-8 juice
1 qt. vodka
2-1/2 tsp. Worcestershire Sauce
5 ozs. "Instant Bar Mix," page 7
2 dashes of Tabasco
salt and pepper
1 lime, thinly sliced

In a large container, combine all ingredients except lime. Pour over block of ice in punch bowl. (You can make your own block by freezing water and garnishes in a container of your choice.) Garnish punch with slices of lime. Serve in punch cups or old- fashioned glasses on-the-rocks. Serves 15 people twice.

BOURBON PUNCH

1 fifth bourbon
4 ozs. dark rum
8 ozs. pineapple juice
8 ozs. grapefruit juice
4 ozs. lemon juice
2 qts. club soda
orange slices and maraschino cherries

Have all ingredients chilled. Mix everything together but club soda. Pour over a block of ice in punch bowl. Just before serving add club soda. Garnish with fruit. Serves 12 people twice.

CELEBRITY PUNCH

2 qts. grape juice
1 pt. orange juice
1 fifth gin
1 qt. gingerale

Combine grape juice, orange juice and gin. Pour over a block of ice in punch bowl. Just before serving add gingerale. Garnish with fruit. Serves 15 people twice.

CHAMPAGNE PUNCH

1 pkg. (13-1/2 ozs.) frozen pineapple
    chunks
1/2 cup sugar
2/3 cup lemon juice
dash of syrup from
    maraschino cherries
1 bottle champagne

Combine all ingredients except champagne and refrigerate. Stir occasionally to make sure pineapple thaws. Just before serving add champagne. Stir and serve in tulip champagne glasses or wine glasses. Serves 4 people twice.

COLD DUCK PUNCH

1 bottle sauterne wine
2 ozs. brandy
1 lemon, squeezed
1/2 orange, squeezed
1 bottle champagne

Into a 1-1/2 gallon container pour sauterne, brandy and juice of lemon and orange. Chill. (This may be frozen in a plastic container and thawed before using.) When ready to serve, pour punch base over ice and add 1 bottle champagne. Serves 6 people twice.

COLD DUCK PUNCH FOR 100

12 bottles sauterne wine
3 cups brandy
12 lemons, squeezed
6 oranges, squeezed
12 bottles dry champagne

Mix wine, brandy and juice together. Pour into six one-half gallon containers and refrigerate. (This may be frozen and thawed before using.) At serving time pour mixture over ice in punch bowl and add champagne.

76

DAIQUIRI PUNCH

1 can (6 ozs.) frozen lemonade
    concentrate
1 can (6 ozs.) frozen limeade
    concentrate
1 fifth white rum
ice cubes

Combine ingredients with a generous amount of ice. Stir well and serve in cocktail glasses, punch cups or old-fashioned glasses. Serves 4 people twice.

FIESTA PUNCH

1 can (6 ozs.) frozen lemonade
    concentrate
1 can (46 ozs.) pineapple juice
2 bottles sauterne wine
1 bottle champagne
block of ice
fruit

Combine lemonade, pineapple juice and sauterne. Chill. Just before serving pour over ice and add champagne. Garnish with fruit. Serves 15 people twice.

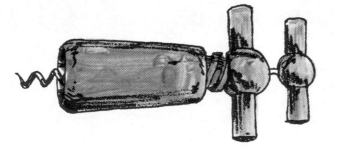

FISH HOUSE PUNCH

A favorite from Colonial times.

1 cup water
5 cups lemon juice
1-1/2 cups sugar
3 pts. dry white wine
1 qt. dark rum
1 qt. light rum
1 qt. brandy
4 ozs. peach brandy
block of ice
1 cup sliced fresh or frozen peaches

Pour water into punch bowl. Add sugar and stir to dissolve. Add lemon juice. Pour in wine, rum, brandy and peach brandy. Let mixture stand at room temperature 2 to 3 hours, stirring occasionally. Before serving add a block of ice to cool. Garnish with peach slices. Serve in punch cups or old-fashioned glasses. Serves 20 people twice.

FRENCH "75" PUNCH

2 bottles champagne
1 fifth brandy
1 qt. club soda

Make an ice ring mold with fruit of your choice. Just before serving pour champagne, brandy and club soda over ice mold. Stir to mix. Serves 12 people twice.

GIN PUNCH

6 ozs. lemon juice
30 ozs. orange juice
1 jigger grenadine
1 fifth gin
1 qt. club soda
fruit slices
block of ice

Pour lemon juice, orange juice, grenadine and gin over a large piece of ice. Just before serving add club soda. Stir and add fruit slices. Serve in punch cups or old-fashioned glasses. Serves 12 people twice.

MAY WINE PUNCH

2 bottles May Wine
1 qt. club soda
1 pkg. (10 ozs.) frozen strawberries,
    thawed

Chill wine and club soda. Just before serving place strawberries in a pitcher. Pour wine and soda over strawberries and stir. Serve in large wine glasses. Serves 12 people twice.

ROSE SPARKLE PUNCH

4 pkgs. (10 ozs. ea.) frozen raspberries,
    thawed
1 cup sugar
4 bottles rosé wine
4 cans (6 oz. ea.) frozen lemonade
    concentrate
2 bottles pink champagne

In a bowl combine raspberries, sugar and one bottle of wine. Cover and let stand at room temperature one hour. Strain mixture into a punch bowl. Add frozen lemonade concentrate. Stir until thawed. Place a block of ice in bowl. Add remaining bottles of wine and champagne. Serve at once. Serves 25 people twice.

RUM PUNCH

4 ozs. pineapple juice
6 ozs. orange juice
6 ozs. lemon juice or lime juice
1 fifth light rum
sugar to taste
block of ice
1 qt. gingerale
fruit

In a large container mix juices, rum and sugar. Chill. Just before serving, pour mixture over a block of ice in punch bowl. Add gingerale and decorate with fruit.

WHISKEY SOUR PUNCH

For a refreshing non-alcoholic punch, omit whiskey.

6 ozs. lemonade concentrate, thawed
24 ozs. orange juice
12 ozs. pineapple juice
sugar to taste
1 fifth whiskey
1 qt. gingerale
orange slices

Combine lemonade and juice. Add sugar and stir to dissolve. Add whiskey and chill. When ready to serve, pour over ice and add gingerale. Float orange slices on top. Serves 12 people twice.

EGGNOG

6 eggs, separated
3/4 cup sugar
1 pt. cream
1 pt. milk
1 oz. dark rum
1 pt. whiskey
nutmeg

Beat whites and yolks seperately. Add 1/2 cup sugar to yolks while beating. Beat whites until stiff, adding 1/4 cup sugar gradually while beating. Fold the yolks into the whites. Add cream and milk. Slowly add rum and whiskey. Stir thoroughly. Serve very cold in a punch cups or old-fashioned glasses. Dust with nutmeg. Serves 10 people twice.

HONOR CUP PUNCH

1 qt. grape juice
2 qts. gingerale or Seven-Up
block of ice

Combine grape juice and gingerale. Serve over ice.

FRUIT PUNCH

6 ozs. lemonade
24 ozs. orange juice
12 ozs. pineapple juice
sugar to taste
1 qt. gingerale

Combine lemonade, juices and sugar. Add gingerale just before serving. Pour over ice and garnish with fruit. Serves 8 people twice.

INDEX TO COCKTAILS SECTION

Champagne and Wine Drinks

After Dinner Drinks

Hot Drinks

Punches

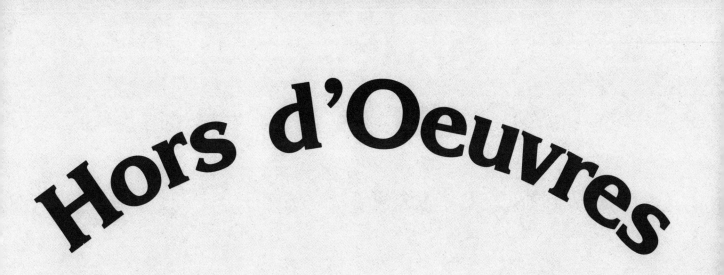

Hors d'Oeuvres

by
Ina C. Boyd

Illustrated by Craig Torlucci

HORS D'OEUVRES SECTION
TABLE OF CONTENTS

See Cocktails Table of Contents
in front of book.

Introduction to Hors d'Oeuvres

The hors d'oeuvres or appetizers served at a party can set the mood for the evening's festivities. Often this opportunity is missed because the hostess or host feels intimidated by imagined difficulties, or misjudges the time required for preparation, thereby leaving a gap in the overall view of the evening. Never again need that important first impression be lessened by unimaginative chips and dips. Easy, but elegant, hors d'oeuvres are conveniently possible for all.

A gathering of friends for a party, a quiet intimate dinner or an early get together before dining out, are all occasions which welcome cocktails and delicious hors d'oeuvres. With this in mind, exceptional cuisine, eye appeal and ease of preparation are the aims of this book. Most recipes can be prepared in advance allowing everyone to relax and enjoy the gathering.

It is my desire that every recipe you try will be pleasing and that you will enjoy using this book many times for many happy occasions.

Ina C. Boyd

hot Hors D'Oeuvres Meat

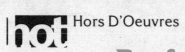
Beef and Cheese on Rye Rounds

3/4 lb. extra lean ground sirloin
3 tbs. catsup
1 tbs. instant minced onion
1 loaf party rye bread
1 pkg. (8 ozs.) Jack cheese.

Combine beef, catsup and onion. Spread mixture on rye rounds and top with a slice of Jack cheese. Bake at 350°F. for 10 minutes then broil until bread is lightly toasted. Keep warm on a hot tray. These can be made in advance, frozen, and taken out as needed; or, they can be made early in the day and refrigerated until ready to serve. Serves 4 to 6 guests.

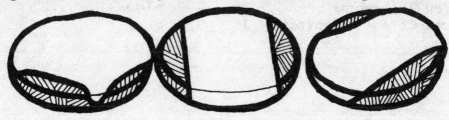

Bacon and Cream Cheese Wraps

Pieces of bread spread with cream cheese and wrapped in crisp bacon make outstanding cocktail fare. Bulk cream cheese is exceptionally good and is best to use if available. Make plenty as they are sensational!

1 pkg. (8 ozs.) cream cheese	12 slices soft white bread
2 tbs. cream or milk	1 pkg. (1 lb.) bacon

With an electric mixer whip cream cheese and cream together. Remove crusts from bread by stacking and cutting 4 slices at a time. Spread cream cheese mixture on each slice. Cut the slices in half, then cut each half into three pieces. Also, cut bacon in 2-1/2 to 3-inch strips. Roll each piece of bread jelly roll fashion with the filling on the inside. Wrap a piece of bacon around each roll. Make sure bacon completely covers the seam so cream cheese will not seep out. Secure with toothpick. (These can be refrigerated or frozen at this stage.) Before serving broil until bacon is crisp. Keep hot on warming tray. Serves 4 to 6 guests.

Tiny Beef Teriyaki

Beef teriyaki served on long bamboo skewers is a welcomed treat on any table. The cocktail hibachi adds to the presentation of this hors d'oeuvre, but if you don't have one don't let that discourage you. Broil and use a hot tray to keep the strips warm. Everyone will feast upon these!

bamboo skewers	1 tbs. honey
1-1/2 lbs. top sirloin	1 tsp. ginger
1/2 cup soy sauce	1/4 tsp. garlic salt
2 tbs. corn oil	

Soak bamboo skewers in water for 1-1/2 hours to prevent them from burning. Partially freeze meat, then slice into very thin slices. Combine remaining ingredients. Marinate meat 1 hour, stirring occasionally. Thread meat slices on soaked skewers. Broil and serve or keep warm on hot tray. Serves 8 guests.

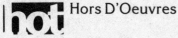

Skewered Beef Strips

This piquant treatment of beef has enough of a bite to require a nice tall drink as an accompaniment.

meat tenderizer
1 lb. (1-in. thick) London Broil
1/2 cup soy sauce
1 tbs. molasses

1 tbs. sesame oil
2 cloves garlic, crushed
1 tbs. Madeira wine
1/2 tsp. coarsely ground black pepper

Sprinkle meat tenderizer on London Broil. Partially freeze meat, then slice into strips about 1/8-inch thick. In a mixing bowl combine soy sauce, molasses, sesame oil, garlic, Madeira and pepper. Add beef strips and mix thoroughly so beef strips are well coated with sauce. Marinate for 1/2 hour. Place on bamboo skewers which have been soaked in water about 1-1/2 hours to prevent them from burning. Broil 2 to 3 minutes on each side. Serve hot. Serves 8 guests.

Marinated Beef Chunks

Sheer sorcery! Tenderized by bottled salad dressing, simple stew beef chunks become a delicious appetizer. They will vanish like magic.

1 lb. stewing beef chunks
1 bottle (8 ozs.) Wishbone Russian dressing
dash of garlic salt
1/2 tsp. tarragon

Cut beef into bite-sized cubes, removing all pieces of fat. Place meat in a 9 x 12-inch baking pan (or something similar so it will fit in one layer). Add as much dressing as is necessary (about 1/2 bottle) to cover the meat. Sprinkle with garlic salt and tarragon. Marinate for several hours. Skewer beef chunks. If using bamboo skewers, soak them in water 1-1/2 hours to prevent them from burning. You may choose to broil the meat and then reheat on a cocktail hibachi, or you may broil it just before guests arrive and keep warm on a hot tray. Serves 4 to 6 guests.

Chafing Dish Tenderloin

For a little gastronomic razzle-dazzle, here is your dish! This kind of tender-loving-care will be appreciated by all.

2 lbs. tenderloin	Madeira Sauce	Bearnaise Sauce, page 11

Just before serving, broil meat on both sides to medium rare. Remove to cutting board and cut into 1-inch cubes. Keep warm in a chafing dish or on a hot tray. Serve with cocktail picks and Madeira Sauce and Bearnaise Sauce for dipping. Serves 6 to 8 guests.

Madeira Sauce

2 tbs. shallots	1 can (15 ozs.) beef gravy	1 tbs. cognac
2 tbs. butter	1/2 cup Madeira wine	

Saute shallots in butter until tender. Add gravy, Madeira and cognac. Simmer for a few minutes. Serve in a sauce warmer, or in a dish on hot tray.

Cheese Meatballs with Bearnaise Sauce

Serve the delicious meatballs alone or with this fabulous dip . . . a great combination that triumphs at any cocktail gathering.

Bearnaise Sauce, page 11
1 lb. extra-lean ground sirloin
1 cup fine dry bread crumbs
1/2 cup Borden's Parmesan and
   Romano cheese
1 tbs. dried parsley

1/8 tsp. instant minced garlic
6 tbs. milk
2 eggs
1-1/2 tsp. salt
1/8 tsp. pepper

Prepare sauce as directed. Combine meatball ingredients in a bowl. Mix together thoroughly. Shape into small cocktail meatballs. Just before serving bake in 350°F. oven 15 to 20 minutes, or until nicely browned. Turn several times during baking. Serve in a chafing dish or in a container on a hot tray with the Bearnaise in a sauce warmer. Serve with foodpicks. To make meatballs ahead, freeze them, uncooked, on a cookie sheet. Transfer to a plastic bag and store in freezer until needed. Bake without defrosting.

Bearnaise Sauce

1-1/4 sticks (10 tbs.) butter
4 egg yolks
1/8 tsp. salt
1/8 tsp. pepper
2 tbs. lemon juice

1/2 cup white wine
2 tbs. tarragon vinegar
1/2 tsp. dried tarragon
1 tbs. chopped shallots

Melt butter over low heat. Place egg yolks, lemon juice, salt and pepper in blender container. Add hot, melted butter. Cover and blend on high speed. Boil wine, vinegar, tarragon and shallots until liquid is reduced to about 1/4 cup. Pour mixture into blender container. Cover and blend on high speed. Serve with meatballs. Sauce can be made a couple of hours ahead and kept warm in a thermos or at room temperature and re-warmed by placing in warm, not hot, water just before serving. (Bearnaise Sauce should be served warm, not hot.) If it should curdle, add a few drops of white wine and blend on high speed a few seconds.

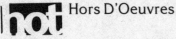
Sweet and Sour Meatballs

An hors d'oeuvre cookbook is hardly complete without a sweet and sour meatball recipe. They are great for a cocktail party and freeze well.

2 lbs. extra lean ground beef
1 egg, slightly beaten
3 tbs. dehydrated onion
1 can (16 ozs.) jellied cranberry sauce
1/4 to 1/2 cup catsup
garlic salt to taste

Combine ground beef, egg and onion. Shape into small balls. Place in a roasting pan and bake in 350°F. oven 15 to 20 minutes or until done. While the meatballs are baking, make the sauce. Mix cranberry sauce, catsup (taste for sweet and sour) and garlic salt in saucepan. Place over low heat and stir until cranberry sauce is melted. Add meatballs and simmer a few minutes to blend flavors. Serve in a chafing dish, or on a hot tray. Makes 40 to 50 meatballs.

Mini-Reuben Sandwiches

The Reuben is easy to make and always enjoys a good reputation. Try making half with just the corned beef and Gruyere cheese, and the other half the more traditional way, with sauerkraut. Each will earn raves.

1 cup well-drained sauerkraut
1/4 tbs. chopped, mild onion
softened butter
1 loaf party rye bread

1/2 lb. corned beef, sliced very thin
Russian dressing
1/2 lb. Gruyere cheese

Combine drained kraut and onion until well mixed. Butter both sides of bread slices. For half of hors de'oeuvres, place ingredients on bottom slice of bread in this order: corned beef, Russian dressing, kraut mixture and cheese. Use only corned beef and cheese on the other half. Top with remaining slices of bread and grill slowly until cheese melts and bread browns. Cut in half and serve. These can be made ahead and grilled just before serving. Keep warm on a hot tray. Serves 6 to 8 guests.

Mini-Ham and Cheese Turnovers

The ideal in entertaining is to prepare ahead so the host and hostess can relax and enjoy the party too. Make these ahead and freeze.

40 onion-flavored crackers	2 tbs. mayonnaise
1 cup all-purpose flour	1 tbs. chopped chives
1/2 cup margarine	1 cup chopped cooked ham
4 ozs. cream cheese	1/4 cup grated Gruyere
2 hard-cooked eggs, chopped	2 eggs, beaten
1/4 cup crumbled cooked bacon	

Crumble crackers into blender container. Add flour and blend. Pour into mixing bowl. Cut in margarine and cream cheese. Form into ball. Wrap and chill. Combine eggs, bacon, mayonnaise, chives, chopped ham and Gruyere. Roll dough 1/8-inch thick. Cut into 2-inch circles. Place 1/2 teaspoon of filling on one-half of each circle. Fold and press edges together. Brush tops with egg. Bake on greased cookie sheet in 400°F. oven 10 to 15 minutes or until golden. Serve warm. Serves 6 to 8 guests.

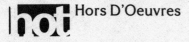
Won Tons

1 can (5 ozs.) water chestnuts
1 lb. ground pork
1 tsp. chopped scallions
2 tbs. soy sauce
1/2 tbs. Madeira wine

1/2 tsp. garlic salt
1/4 tsp. seasoned salt
1 lb. won ton skins
1 egg, beaten

Coarsely grind chestnuts. Mix with pork, scallions, soy sauce, Madeira, garlic salt and seasoned salt. Cut won ton skins into 2-inch squares. Keep skins covered with a damp cloth. Dip fingers into water and wet edges of each square as you work with it. Place a small amount of filling in the center of square. Fold in half, top to bottom. Press edges together. Moisten top left corner with beaten egg. Bring top left corner under top right corner. Press to seal. Fry won tons in hot oil until golden. Serve with a cocktail sauce and a sweet and sour sauce. Serves 6 guests.

Chinese Spareribs

It used to be an expensive luxury to have meats specially prepared at a small butcher's shop. Today more and more supermarkets are offering this personalized convenience. Take advantage of this opportunity, and all you have to do is make the sauce for this all-time favorite—Chinese spareribs. Add a Polynesian drink, and you'll have an exceptional cocktail hour.

2-1/2 to 3 lbs. spareribs
1/4 cup dark molasses
3 tbs. hoisin sauce
2 tbs. Madeira wine

1 tsp. garlic salt
2 tbs. honey
2 tbs. soy sauce
1/2 tsp. red food coloring (optional)

Boil spareribs in large pot of water 15 to 20 minutes to reduce fat. Drain and dry ribs on paper towels. Combine remaining ingredients. Brush sauce on both sides of spareribs. Place meat side down in a shallow baking pan. Bake in 350°F. oven 1/2 hour. Pour off fat and turn ribs over. Brush sauce on top side. Bake for another 1/2 hour at 325°F. Serves 4 to 6 guests.

17

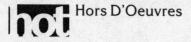
Pork Kabobs

Small chunks of pork tenderloin brushed with this tangy sauce contribute a bit of the unusual to your nibbler's selection. They can be prepared ahead and warmed on a hibachi or hot tray. They're simply delicious!

1-1/2 lbs. pork tenderloin
1/4 cup French dressing
1/2 tsp. curry powder
1 tbs. dijon-style mustard
1/4 cup barbeque sauce

3 tbs. vermouth
1/4 tsp. rosemary
garlic salt to taste
pepper

Cut pork into 1-inch cubes. Place in bowl. Combine French dressing, curry powder, mustard, barbeque sauce, vermouth, rosemary, garlic salt, and pepper. Pour mixture over pork and marinate 2 hours. Thread marinated pork on skewers and broil or barbeque about 15 minutes. Turn and brush with the marinade several times during cooking. Keep warm on a hot tray or cocktail hibachi. Serves 4 to 6 guests.

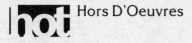

Skewered Lamb

Enjoy your next leg of lamb twice. Before roasting the whole leg, cut off one pound for making appetizers. Few can resist this unusual and delectable hors d'oeuvre. You will need a Chinese grocery or gourmet food store for the sesame oil and hoisin sauce. Then it's simply a matter of marinating, broiling and relishing!

1 lb. lamb from leg
1 tbs. soy sauce
1 tbs. brown sugar
2 tbs. corn or peanut oil

1 tsp. sesame oil
2 tbs. hoisin sauce
1/4 tsp. garlic salt
dash of pepper

Slice lamb in small pieces. Combine remaining ingredients and marinate lamb for several hours. Before company arrives skewer lamb on bamboo skewers which have been soaked in water for 1-1/2 hours to prevent them from burning. Just before serving, broil lamb, turning until browned on each side. Serve on cocktail hibachi or hot tray. Serves 4 to 6 guests.

Meat-Stuffed Mushrooms

The marvelous mushroom is a real addition to the hors d'oeuvre circuit. It serves as the delectable container for a great variety of fillings. This ground beef mixture tastes very special in mushrooms.

3/4 lb. extra lean ground beef
3 tbs. catsup
1 tbs. instant minced onion
1 lb. mushrooms
1/2 lb. Jack cheese

Combine beef, catsup and onion. Remove stems from mushrooms. Clean caps by wiping with a damp paper towel. Fill caps with meat mixture. Make half plain, and half with the Jack cheese placed on top of the filling. Bake in a 350°F. oven 15 minutes or until done. These can be made and frozen before cooking. Place on a cookie tray, freeze and then transfer to a plastic bag. They can also be made early in the day and refrigerated until ready to bake. Keep warm on a hot tray. Serves 4 to 6 guests.

Pizza-Style Mushrooms

If you are a "Pepperoni Pizza Lover," and even if not, these will be a favorite. Make ahead and freeze, then enjoy the raves.

1 to 1-1/2 lbs. large mushrooms
2 tbs. butter or margarine
1 onion, finely chopped
1 clove garlic, finely chopped
2 tbs. finely chopped green pepper
2 ozs. pepperoni, diced

1/4 cup chicken broth
1/2 cup soft bread crumbs
3 tbs. Borden's Parmesan and
   Romano Cheese
Dash each salt, pepper and oregano
1 pkg. sliced mozzarella cheese

Clean mushrooms. Remove stems and chop finely. Melt butter in an electric frying pan. Saute onion, garlic, green pepper, pepperoni and mushroom stems. Cook until soft. Add chicken broth, bread crumbs (made in blender), Parmesan and Romano Cheese and seasonings. Cook until liquid is absorbed. Stuff mixture into mushroom caps. Top with mozzarella cheese that has been cut to fit the top of the mushroom cap. Bake in 325°F. oven 20 minutes. Serves 6 guests.

21

Cocktail Dogs

The hot dog has a definite role in the American scene and this sweet and sour treatment will make it very much a part of the cocktail scene.

1 pkg. (16 ozs.) extra-mild, skinless weiners
2 tbs. chopped onion
3/4 cup currant jelly
3/4 cup chili sauce
1/2 tsp. dijon mustard
1 can (13-1/2 ozs.) pineapple chunks, drained
1/4 tsp. garlic salt

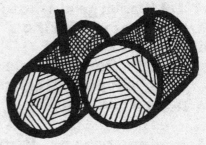

Slice weiners on the diagonal, 1/2-inch thick. Saute until lightly browned and cooked through. Add onion and saute until limp. In a separate pan combine remaining ingredients for sauce. Bring to boil slowly. Add onions and weiners and heat together thoroughly. Keep warm in chafing dish and serve with toothpicks. Serves 8 to 10 guests.

Taco Beef Dip

If you have an affinity for tacos, dote on this piquant dip. Make it early in the day and heat just before serving . . . then wait for resounding oles! Teenagers enjoy this so it's an ideal choice for family entertaining.

1 lb. extra lean ground beef
1 pkg. (1-1/4 ozs.) taco seasoning
1/2 cup water
1/2 cup beer

6 tbs. (1/2 6-oz. can) tomato taste
1 cup (4 ozs.) grated cheddar cheese
3 to 4 pkgs. (5-1/2 ozs. ea.) tortilla chips

Brown beef and break into bits. Drain off fat. Add taco seasoning. Stir in water, beer and tomato paste. Simmer, covered, 10 minutes. Transfer mixture to two onion soup bowls or ramekins. Add half of grated cheese to each bowl. Bake in 325°F. oven 5 to 10 minutes. Serve just warm, using tortilla chips for dipping—assist with a spreading knife. Serve about 2 packages of tortilla chips with each bowl of dip. This mixture freezes well. Serves 6 to 8 guests.

hot Hors D'Oeuvres Poultry

Crispy Chicken Wings

This is sure to earn the "clean plate award" at your next cocktail gathering. Your butcher may sell "Hors d'oeuvre chicken wings;" they're like tiny drumsticks. That makes preparing this delicious cocktail accompaniment a breeze.

3 lbs. chicken wings
1/3 cup white wine
2/3 cup corn oil
1 pkg. (.07 oz.) Good Seasons Garlic Salad Dressing mix

If chicken wings are not already prepared, cut off tips and discard. Cut remaining wings in half and place in a Pyrex baking dish. Combine wine, oil and dressing mix. Pour over chicken wings and marinate for several hours. When ready to cook, place in a large baking pan. Bake in 325°F. oven 15 to 20 minutes. Turn and brush with the marinade. Bake 15 to 20 minutes longer. Then broil on both sides until crispy. The wings can be prepared up to the point of broiling early in the day. Serves 6 to 8 guests.

Polynesian Chicken Wings

Another fabulous tidbit. Don't be frightened by thoughts of messy fingers. These are very tiny, easily handled, and luscious.

3 lbs. chicken wings
1 cup soy sauce
1/2 cup orange juice
1/2 cup pineapple juice
1/4 cup lemon juice
1/4 cup Madeira wine
3 cloves garlic
1 tbs. honey

If wings are not already prepared, cut off tips and discard. Cut remaining wings in half. Place in Pyrex baking dish. Combine remaining ingredients and pour over wings. Let marinate several hours. When ready to cook, place wings in a large baking pan. Bake in 325°F. oven for 1 hour, then broil on both sides untl crispy. Serves 6 to 8 guests.

Chicken Teriyaki Strips

This is an unusual and delectable marinade for chicken. The addition of mandarin oranges lends color to the hors d'oeuvre table. Pamper your guests and accompany this with a Polynesian-type drink. The consensus will be . . . encore!

1 can (11 ozs.) mandarin oranges
1-1/2 lbs. boneless chicken breasts
1/2 cup soy sauce
1/8 tsp. instant minced garlic
2 tsp. maple syrup

1/4 cup water
1/4 cup wine vinegar
1/4 cup Madeira wine
3 tbs. applesauce
1/4 tsp. ginger

Drain oranges. Cut chicken into chunks or cubes. Combine remaining ingredients and pour over chicken. Marinate for 1/2 to 1 hour. Skewer chicken cubes, alternating with orange segments. Broil for a few minutes on each side, turning skewers to cook evenly. Brush several times with marinade. For best results broil just before serving so chicken does not become dry. Keep warm on a hot tray. Serves 4 to 6 guests.

Chicken Liver Surprises

This is an interesting variation for chicken livers. It is a compatable trio and very easy to prepare. Make early in the day and bake. Refrigerate until just before cocktail time and reheat under the broiler.

1 lb. chicken livers
1 lb. bacon
1 jar sweet-pickled watermelon rind

Cut chicken livers into chunks and bacon into 2-1/2 to 3 inch strips. Wrap a piece of liver and a cube of watermelon rind with bacon. Secure with a foodpick. Bake in 325°F. oven until bacon and chicken livers are cooked. Place under broiler to crisp bacon. Serve on hot tray. Serves 6 to 8 guests.

hot Hors D'Oeuvres Seafood

31

Scampi

Appetizers should delight the taste buds but not spoil the appetite. You may be sure of delighting your guests with this treatment of shrimp.

1 pkg. (16 ozs.) frozen, uncooked shrimp, defrosted
3/4 cup Madeira wine
1 stick margarine or butter
2 tbs. shallots
2 tbs. parsley
1 tbs. lemon juice

Butterfly shrimp by splitting each one almost in two. Melt margarine in fry pan. Saute shallots. Add shrimp and cook until pink. Stir in lemon juice, parsley and Madeira. Bring to a boil and cook until wine is reduced. Serve in a dish with lemon wedges. Keep warm on hot tray. Serves 4 to 6 guests.

Fried Shrimp

Subtly-flavored, light, crispy-fried shrimp is a true culinary art! Show your kitchen wizardry using this simple recipe to produce a delectable morsel. These are a luxury! Serve with both cocktail sauce and a sweet and sour sauce.

1 pkg. (16 ozs.) frozen, uncooked shrimp
garlic salt
1 cup flour
1/4 cup cornstarch
1/4 cup crackermeal

1/4 tsp. baking powder
1 egg, slightly beaten
1-1/2 cups water
1/4 cup milk
3/4 cup corn oil

Defrost shrimp and spread out on a flat surface. Very lightly sprinkle with garlic salt so that each is subtly flavored. Combine remaining ingredients except oil. Dip shrimp into batter to lightly cover. Heat oil to 400°F. Fry shrimp until golden brown on each side. Drain on paper towels. Keep warm on a hot tray or in a warming dish. Serves 4 guests.

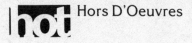

Langostinos

Diversify your cocktail table with these palatable gifts from the sea found in the freezer section of your local market. Your friends will relish this unusual hors d'oeuvre.

1 pkg. (12 ozs.) frozen langostinos
1-1/2 sticks of butter or margarine
1/2 cup vermouth
1/2 cup Ritz Cracker crumbs

1/4 cup Cheese Tidbits, crushed
1/4 tsp. garlic salt
individual sea shells

Saute langastinos in 2 tablespoons butter. Add vermouth and cook until the wine is reduced by at least half. Cream together remaining butter, cracker crumbs and garlic salt. Divide langostinos and wine into individual shells. Top with a scant tablespoon of butter mixture. For ease, make ahead and freeze or make early in the day. Just before serving, bake in 350°F. oven 10 minutes, or until butter has melted and dispersed among the langostinos. Serve each shell on a small cocktail tray with a cocktail fork. Serves 6 to 8 guests.

hot

Croustades With Crabmeat Mornay

Croustades are marvelously simple, yet impressive. Circles of bread shaped into miniature muffin tins can be prepared by even a novice.

14 to 15 slices soft white bread
8 ozs. fresh or frozen crabmeat
2 tbs. butter or margarine
2 tbs. flour
1 cup milk

2 tbs. cubed Gruyere cheese
2 tbs. grated Parmesan or
   Romano cheese
1/2 tsp. salt
1/4 tsp. pepper

Cut circles from bread using a 2-inch cutter or juice glass. You can cut two circles from each piece. Press bread circles into generously buttered miniature muffin tins. Cover with plastic wrap. Melt butter in saucepan. Stir in flour. Gradually add milk while stirring to keep sauce smooth. Add cheese and continue stirring until cheese melts. Stir crabmeat into cheese sauce. (Mixture can be refrigerated at this point.) Spoon a small amount of filling into croustades. Bake in 425°F. oven 15 minutes. Keep warm on hot tray. Serves 6 to 8 guests.

Clams Casino

Add another joy to your beachcombing and consequently to your cocktail hour by collecting shells for this hors d'oeuvre on your next stroll on the beach. This very easy but delicate and flavorful specimen may be made in advance and refrigerated, or frozen. This is a favorite!

1 can (6-1/2 ozs.) chopped clams
1 hard-cooked egg, chopped
1/2 medium onion, chopped
1/2 cup bread crumbs
1/4 cup butter or margarine

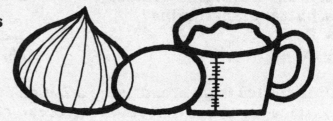

Drain clams, reserving juice. In frying pan saute onion in butter until softened. Add clams, egg and bread crumbs. Moisten with reserved clam juice using about 1/4 to 1/2 of the juice. Spoon mixture into small seafood shells. Broil and serve with cocktail forks. Makes 4 to 6 servings.

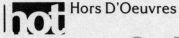

Scallops in White Wine Sauce

A gourmet's delight, simply prepared! Savor this one!

1 lb. scallops	1/4 tsp. dried tarragon
1/2 cup dry vermouth	dash of pepper
1 cup sliced mushrooms	1 cup half and half
2 tbs. finely chopped shallots	4 tbs. butter or margarine
1/4 tsp. salt	1 tbs. flour

Cut scallops into bite-sized pieces. Place in saucepan with vermouth, mushrooms, shallots and seasonings. Bring to boil and simmer 5 minutes. Remove mushrooms and scallops and reduce liquid to half by boiling. Add cream and boil until reduced to a syrupy consistency. Make a paste of flour and butter. Add little by little to thicken cream. Put scallops and mushrooms into individual shells. Pour cream sauce over each portion. These can be made ahead and frozen, or made early in the day. When ready to serve, bake in 350°F. oven about 10 minutes. Serves 4 to 6 guests.

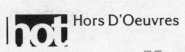
Mushrooms With Escargots

12 large mushroom caps
1 can of snails (12 snails)
1 stick unsalted butter, softened
1 clove garlic, minced
1 tbs. shallots, chopped

1/2 tsp. dried parsley
dash salt and pepper
4 tbs. vermouth
1 loaf Italian bread, thinly sliced

Clean mushrooms and remove stems. Drain and rinse snails. Combine 4 tablespoons softened butter, garlic, shallots, parsley, salt and pepper. Place a little butter mixture in the bottom of each mushroom cap. Fill each cap with a snail and top with more garlic butter. Place 1 tablespoon butter and 1 tablespoon vermouth in the bottom of each of four snail dishes, ramekins or onion soup bowls. Arrange 3 filled mushrooms in each dish. Bake in 400°F. oven 8 to 10 minutes. Before serving, spoon sauce on bottom of each dish over snails and mushrooms for extra flavor. Accompany with bread and cocktail forks. These can be prepared ahead to the point of baking. Serves 4 guests.

Stuffed Mussels St. Jacques

2 lbs. mussels
1 cup white wine
1/4 cup water
1/2 cup butter or margarine
2 cups bread crumbs

2 tbs. shallots
1/2 medium tomato
2 tsp. lemon juice
1/2 lb. butter
2 cloves garlic, crushed

Clean and scrub mussels. Steam in wine and water until they open. Discard any that do not open. Rinse with cold water. Completely open shells and throw away the empty half. In butter or margarine, saute shallots until tender. Make fresh bread crumbs in blender. Remove crumbs from blender and puree tomato. Combine bread crumbs, tomato puree, lemon juice and sauteed shallots. Spoon over mussels. Place 5 to 6 stuffed mussels in individual ramekins. Bake in 400°F. oven 10 minutes. In the meantime, heat butter and garlic together. Pour a small amount of garlic butter into the bottom of each ramekin for dipping mussels. Serve with cocktail forks. Serves 8 to 10 guests.

hot Hors D'Oeuvres Cheese

Toasted Cheese Rounds

Hot canapes infer kitchen bondage, but this need not be true with to-day's many conveniences. This mixture can be prepared in advance and spread before your company arrives. It's a triumphant combination, yet very simple. The aroma alone is a teaser!

1/4 cup grated mozzarella cheese
1/3 cup Borden's Parmesan and Romano cheese
3/4 cup mayonnaise
1/2 cup chopped red onion
1 loaf party rye bread

Mix the cheeses, mayonnaise and onion. Spread on rye rounds. Broil until bubbly. Keep warm on hot tray. Serves 4 to 6 guests.

Mini-Pizzas on Party Rye

Luscious, chewy mozzarella cheese melts in your mouth with this favorite. The next time you prepare spaghetti sauce, save some in the freezer for it will make this hors d'oeuvre uniquely yours.

1 midget salami roll
1 loaf party rye bread
2/3 cup of your favorite spaghetti sauce
1 pkg. (8 ozs.) mozzarella cheese
oregano

Cut thin slices of salami roll and place on rye rounds. Spread about 1/2 teaspoon spaghetti sauce on salami. Top with a slice of mozzarella cheese. Sprinkle oregano on the cheese. Bake in 325°F. oven about 10 minutes or until cheese melts. Serves 4 to 6 guests.

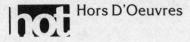

Cheese Melts

Melba toast rounds are receptacles for zestfully flavored cheese. They are truly "melt in your mouth" morsels.

2 hard-cooked eggs
7 strips bacon
2 tbs. finely chopped onion
1 jar (8 ozs.) Cheese Whiz
1/8 tsp. cayenne pepper
1/8 tsp. garlic salt
plain melba rounds

Chop eggs finely. Cook bacon until very crisp. Crumble into small pieces. In a bowl, combine chopped eggs, bacon, onion, Cheese Whiz and seasonings. Mix well. Spread melba rounds with mixture and place on cookie sheet. Bake in 400°F. oven until cheese melts. Serves 4 to 6 guests.

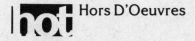
Quiche Nibbler

Great for Sunday brunch, and it can be created very easily. Refrigerated crescent dinner rolls provide instant crust.

1 can (8 ozs.) Pillsbury Crescent Rolls
1/2 lb. bacon
1/2 cup chopped onion
1-1/2 cups cubed Gruyere cheese
8 egg yolks

2 cups half and half or cream
1/4 tsp. <u>each</u> salt,
    dry mustard and nutmeg
1/8 tsp. pepper

Preheat oven to 375°F. Separate crescent dough into two large rectangles. Place on ungreased 15 x 10-inch jelly roll pan. Gently press dough to cover bottom and edges of pan. Seal perforations. Cook onion and bacon. Drain and crumble bacon. Distribute onions, bacon and Gruyere evenly over dough. Combine egg yolks, half and half, mustard, nutmeg, salt and pepper. Pour over ingredients in crust. Bake in 375°F. oven 25 to 30 minutes, or until knife inserted into custard comes out clean. Let stand 5 minutes before cutting into small squares. Serves 8 to 10 guests.

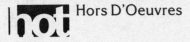

Zucchini Rounds

Zucchini on the hors d'oeuvre platter not only provides a distinctive variation, but is another delightful way to deplete an abundant crop.

2 lbs. small zucchini
1/4 lb. margarine
1/4 lb. sharp cheddar cheese, grated
1 pkg. (3 ozs.) cream cheese
2 egg whites

Slice zucchini on the diagonal. In a saucepan, heat butter and cheeses until melted. Whip the egg whites until stiff. Whisk into butter and cheese mixture. Cool and spread generously on zucchini. Bake in 375°F. oven about 20 minutes. Serve warm. Serves 6 to 8 guests.

Hot Cheese and Sausage Puffs

These are mouthwatering for any occasion and especially ideal for brunch. They are easily made ahead of time, ready to be popped into the oven at the last minutes . . . the hostess' greatest ally.

1 jar (5 ozs.) Olde English Cheese Spread
1 cup flour
1/4 lb. margarine
1/2 tsp. garlic salt
1/4 tsp. seasoned salt
6 ozs. regular bulk pork sausage

Mix cheese spread, flour, margarine and salt together well. Divide mixture in half and add sausage to one half. Shape both mixtures into 1/2-inch balls. Chill. Bake in 350°F. oven 15 minutes. Serve on a hot tray to keep warm. Serves 4 to 6 guests.

hot Hors D'Oeuvres Other Delights

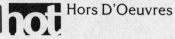

Onion-Buttered Tidbits

Here's an unusual treat that is truly delectable and guaranteed to enhance your reputation as a hostess. Cheers for convenience foods that add elegance to our tables, yet demand little of a busy hostess. These subtly-flavored, crispy bites, made from pita bread (sometimes called pocket bread) disappear fast.

1 env. Lipton Onion Soup mix
1/2 tsp. chopped parsley

2-1/2 sticks margarine, softened
1 pkg. (4) large pita breads

Combine soup mix, parsley and softened margarine. Cut pita breads into bite-size wedges. Separate tops from bottoms. Lightly spread seasoned butter on the inner sides. Bake in 325°F. oven until crispy, about 10 minutes. Watch carefully. Serve on hot tray to keep warm. These can be made in advance and frozen before baking. Freeze flat on a cookie sheet, then transfer to a large plastic bag. (Extra onion-butter may be refrigereated for at least two weeks.) Serves 8 to 10 guests.

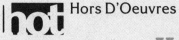

Herb-Buttered Triangles

Here's an ideal hors d'oeuvre to serve before a large meal. It is light and crispy . . . truly a nibbler's delight!

1 pkg. (4) large pita breads	1 tsp. lemon juice
1/2 cup margarine	1/4 tsp. Worcestershire sauce
1/2 tsp. dijon mustard	1/4 tsp. garlic salt
1/2 tsp. sweet basil	

Cut pita breads as described in Onion-Buttered Tidbits on page 50. Mix remaining ingredients and spread on inner sides of triangles. Bake until crisp in 325°F. oven, about 8 to 10 minutes. Watch carefully. Can be made ahead, and freeze well.

Garlic Cheese Triangles — Combine 1/4 cup margarine, 1 teaspoon garlic salt and 2 cups (8 ozs.) grated New York cheddar cheese. Lightly spread mixture on inner sides of triangles. Bake as directed above.

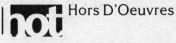
Mushrooms With Stuffing

Here's to the mushroom . . . the perfect bite-size hors d'oeuvre caddy! Pepperidge Farm Stuffing flavored with shallots and a hint of garlic seasoning is a triumphant combination. Your friends will relish these and you will, too. They can be prepared ahead of time and frozen. Heat when needed. They're delectable!

1 lb. large fresh mushrooms
2 tbs. chopped shallots
6 tbs. margarine or butter

1 cup Pepperidge Farm
   Herb-Seasoned Stuffing mix
1/2 cup chicken broth
1/4 tsp. garlic salt

Clean mushrooms and remove stems. Saute chopped stems and shallots in 4 tablespoons margarine. Stir in stuffing, chicken broth and garlic salt. Stuff mushrooms with mixture and place in a Pyrex pie plate with 2 tablespoons margarine. These may be prepared ahead and refrigerated, or frozen. When ready to serve, bake in 350°F. oven 20 minutes or until done. Serves 4 to 6 guests.

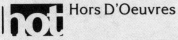
Onion Pie With Ham Crust

This is a change from the traditional quiche and a mouthwatering one at that! The ham crust accommodates carmelized onions which have been simmered in wine . . . a delectable flavor!

1 lb. boiled ham	1/2 tsp. sugar
3 tbs. butter	3 ozs. white wine
1 tbs. corn oil	3 eggs
4 red onions, sliced	1 cup cream
salt and pepper	1/4 tsp. nutmeg

Grind ham in blender or food processor. Press ground ham into a 9-inch Pyrex pie plate to form the crust. Saute onions in butter and oil until translucent and tender. Add salt, pepper and sugar. Cook about 15 minutes. Add wine and simmer 10 minutes longer. Beat eggs with cream and nutmeg. Add to onions. Pour onion mixture into ham shell. Bake in 375°F. oven 25 to 30 minutes. Cut into small slices and serve on little hors d'oeuvres trays with cocktail forks. Serves 10 to 12 guests.

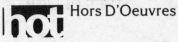

Hot Mushroom Turnovers

These are exceptional and the flavor is enhanced when they are made ahead, which makes their preparation ideal. You'll enjoy the luxury of serving warm pastries with ease. The cream cheese pastry is easy to work with as well as being a delicious encasement for the savory filling

Cream Cheese Pastry, page 55
3 tbs. margarine
3 tbs. finely minced shallots
1/2 lb. mushrooms, finely minced
1/2 tsp. salt

1/4 tsp. nutmeg
1/4 tsp. thyme
2 tbs. flour
1/4 cup sour cream

Prepare pastry as directed. Melt margarine in frying pan. Saute shallots and mushrooms until tender. Stir in seasonings and flour. Blend in sour cream. Let cool. When ready to make turnovers, bring dough to room temperature. Roll out half of the dough at a time on a floured board. Roll thin and cut 2-inch circles with cookie cutter or jelly glass. Brush edge of circles with beaten egg. Place 1/2 teaspoon mushroom mixture on each

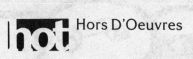

pastry circle. Fold in half to form tart. Press edges together with fork and prick tops of tarts. Brush with beaten egg. Place on ungreased cookie sheet. Bake in 450°F. oven 12 to 15 minutes. Flavor is improved if turnovers are baked and frozen, then reheated just before serving. Keep warm on hot tray. Serves 8 guests.

Cream Cheese Pastry

8 ozs. bulk or packaged cream cheese
1/2 cup margarine
1-1/2 cups flour

Mix ingredients together well. Wrap in waxed paper and refrigerate at least 1 hour or overnight if desired.

cold | Hors D'Oeuvres Meat

French Country Pâté

Pâté is frequently considered synonymous with liver. However this is a classic country pâté made with ground veal and ground pork. If you have your butcher prepare the meat, the pâté is easy to make . . . one step at a time. No additional hors d'oeuvres are necessary as this is a treat to be savored. It makes a lovely first course for a dinner party.

1 lb. bacon
3/4 lb. thickly sliced boiled ham
1/4 cup finely chopped shallots
2 tbs. butter or margarine
1/2 cup Madeira wine
1 lb. ground pork
1 lb. ground veal

1/2 lb. ground pork fat
1/2 tsp. thyme
1/2 tsp. sweet basil
1/2 tsp. garlic salt
dash allspice, salt and pepper
2 eggs, lightly beaten
1 bay leaf

Buy an inexpensive, fatty bacon as the fat is what you want. Avoid a strong smokey-flavored bacon. Line the bottom and sides of a loaf pan with bacon so that pieces extend over the four sides of the pan. Set aside. Cut ham in 1/4 inch strips. Saute shallots in butter until tender. Add Madeira and boil until reduced by half. Transfer shallots and wine to mixing bowl. Add pork, veal, pork fat, thyme, basil, garlic salt, allspice, salt, pepper and eggs. Mix well. Place a third of the mixture in the bottom of bacon-lined pan. Cover with half the ham strips. Add another third of mixture, then the remaining ham. Cover ham with remaining meat mixture. Lay bay leaf on top and cover with extended bacon strips. Cover pan with aluminum foil and a heavy cover. Set in larger pan. Add about an inch of boiling water. Bake in 350°F. oven 1-1/2 hours. Remove from oven and place loaf pan on a plate. On top of the foil covering, but resting against the pâté, place a piece of wood (a small cutting board will do). On it place a heavy object such as a rock or parts of a meat grinder. This will pack the pâté so there will be no air spaces. Allow the pâté to cool at room temperature for several hours or overnight. Then chill with the weight still on. To serve, slice pâté in thin slices and remove bacon fat. Serve on little hors d'oeuvre trays with small forks, offering small pieces of French bread as an accompaniment.

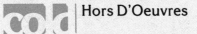

Easy Pâté

It's always a joy to see guests enjoy your offerings with gusto. It's even more satisfying when the preparation has been easy. Relish this one!

**1/2 lb. liverwurst
2 tbs. finely chopped onion
mayonnaise
1/2 lb. bulk cream cheese
2 tbs. milk or cream
chopped chives**

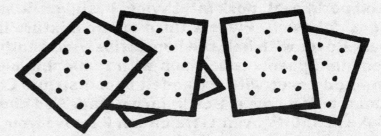

In blender mix liverwurst until smooth. Add chopped onion and enough mayonnaise to give good flavor and enough consistency to shape. Line a bowl with clear plastic wrap. Pack the liverwurst mixture into bowl using excess plastic wrap to cover top. Chill 2 hours. Turn liverwurst mold upside down onto a plate and remove plastic wrap. Whip cream cheese and cream together with a mixer. Frost pâté with cream cheese and cover top with chopped chives. Serve with crackers, melba toast or melba rounds.

Rillettes

This subtle delicacy is a wonderful holiday tradition.

3 lbs. lean pork

2 lbs. pork fat slices

4 to 5 slices cooked turkey

2 tsp. salt

1 tsp. pepper

1 clove garlic, crushed

1/2 tsp. thyme

1/4 tsp. nutmeg

1 bay leaf

3/4 cup water

Cut pork in cubes and place in crockery cooker. Cover with fat slices. Place turkey slices over fat. Add salt, pepper, garlic, thyme, nutmeg, bay leaf and water. Cook on low all day. Strain off liquid and fat into two separate containers and save. With two forks, shred meat while still hot. Pack into small crocks. When crocks are half filled, spoon some of the juices and fat on top and blend into mixture. Finish filling crocks and repeat process. Seal tops of crocks with fat. Refrigerate. When ready to serve remove fat and let spread come to room temperature. Serve with mild Bremner Wafers. Makes about 3 cups.

Chopped Chicken Liver Spread

Chopped chicken liver spread has become a favorite hors d'oeuvre. Your guests will relish this delicious version.

1 lb. chicken livers	2 hard-cooked eggs
2 tbs. minced shallots	1/8 tsp. nutmeg
3 to 4 tbs. margarine	mayonnaise
1 medium onion, chopped	salt and pepper

Saute chicken livers and shallots in margarine until liver is cooked and shallots are transparent and tender. Let cool. Combine chicken livers, shallots, onion and hard-cooked eggs using a blender or food processor. Add nutmeg, salt and pepper to taste. Moisten with mayonnaise to your personal taste. Refrigerate. Serve cold with freshly made toast points (crusts trimmed) or Melba toast or rounds.

Rolled Ham With Garlic and Herbed Cheese

This interesting treatment of ham will be a popular addition to your cocktail table. Sample and see. The ham should be in thicker slices than used for sandwiches. They will be less apt to tear when spreading with cheese, and be tastier.

Garlic and Herbed Cheese,* page 78
1/2 lb. boiled ham

Let cheese come to room temperature. Spread each slice of ham with cheese mixture and roll up jelly roll fashion. Place in freezer until firm enough to slice but not frozen. Using a sharp knife, slice each roll into 1/4-inch circles. Freeze on a cookie sheet and then store in a plastic bag and remove as needed.

*Boursin cheese may be substituted for Garlic and Herbed Cheese.

Savory Beef Chunks

Another make ahead "bet you can't eat just one" marvel! These can be stored in a covered jar in the refrigerator for weeks . . . depending on how long you can resist them.

1-1/2 lbs. boneless beef shoulder
2 tbs. corn oil
2 tbs. sugar
1/2 cup water
1 tsp. chopped shallots
1 tbs. Galliano
1/4 to 1/2 tsp. cayenne pepper
1/2 tsp. salt
2 tbs. soy sauce
garlic salt

Preheat oven to 200°F. Cut beef into 1/2-inch cubes trimming off all fat. Heat oil in an electric fry pan. Add sugar and beef cubes. Sear and

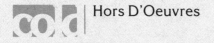
sugar-coat the beef for 4 to 5 minutes. Stir in remaining ingredients except garlic salt. Bring to a boil then reduce heat to medium. Cover and cook 30 minutes, stirring frequently. During the last five minutes remove cover and let liquid evaporate. Transfer beef to a baking sheet and lightly sprinkle with garlic salt. Reduce oven to 175°F. and dry beef for 1 hour. Turn off heat and let beef cubes cool in the oven. Store in a covered container in the refrigerator. Impale beef on foodpicks with various colored frills for an attractive presentation. Garnish with parsley sprigs. Serves 6 to 8 guests.

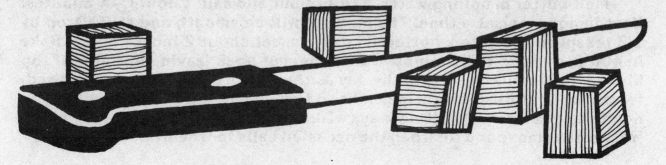

Tiny Cocktail Puffs

These easily made puffs are impressive for a cocktail party. Stuff with chicken, turkey, ham, tuna, crabmeat or salmon filling and watch them disappear.

1/2 cup butter	1/4 to 1/2 tsp. salt
1 cup boiling water	4 eggs
1 cup flour	

Melt butter in boiling water. Stir in flour and salt. Cook 3 – 4 minutes. Beat in eggs, one at a time. The mixture will be smooth and stiff. Drop by 1/2 teaspoonfuls onto a buttered cookie sheet about 2-inches apart. Bake in 400°F. oven 15 to 20 minutes. Cool and cut open leaving one side of top hinged. Don't fill too early in the day as they will become soggy. If desired, freeze for later use. This recipe makes 3 to 4 dozen. Cut recipe in half if you don't want as many. But, it's always a treat to have some tucked away in the freezer to remove and fill when the occasion calls for them.

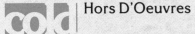
Gruyere Puffs With Corned Beef Filling

For additional interest to your cocktail puff platter, try Gruyere cheese puffs with a tangy corned beef filling.

1/4 lb. Gruyere cheese, grated
Tiny Cocktail Puffs, page 66

Add Gruyere to cheese puffs after eggs have been beaten in. Bake as directed.

Corned Beef Filling

2 cups finely chopped deli-style corned beef
2 tbs. finely chopped onion
1/4 tsp. horseradish

2 to 3 tbs. mustard
2 tsp. mayonnaise

Combine ingredients and fill cheese puffs. Makes 3 to 4 dozen.

cold | Hors D'Oeuvres Seafood

Shrimp Or Crabmeat With Artichokes

Arrange on a wooden tray in sunburst fashion for great eye appeal. It tastes as good as it looks.

2 large artichokes	2 cans (4-1/2 ozs. ea.) small shrimp, drained
Josef's Remoulade Sauce	<u>or</u> 1 pkg. (6 ozs.) frozen crabmeat
mayonnaise	

Trim base of artichokes and snap off the small botton outer leaves. Using a large sharp knife slice about 1-inch off the top. Cut the points off of the rest of the leaves with scissors. Bring about 6 quarts of water to boil. Drop in artichokes and boil them briskly, uncovered, for about 30 minutes, turning occasionally if necessary. They are cooked when their bases are easily pierced with a fork. Drain upside down. Combine 1/2 cup remoulade sauce (found in the gourmet section of your market) and 3 to 4 tablespoons mayonnaise, according to your taste. Peel off the sturdy leaves of the artichokes. Put a small dab of the mixture on the meaty end of each artichoke leaf. Place a shrimp or crab chunk on top of sauce. Serves 4 to 6 guests.

Skewered Shrimp, Avocado and Scallops

A luxurious trio dipped in a sauce that has been tinged with vodka — it's mouthwatering.

1/2 lb. scallops
1 large ripe avocado
lemon juice
butter

1/2 lb. cooked shrimp
1 cup mayonnaise
1 tbs. vodka

Place scallops in a baking pan. Dab with lemon juice and butter. Broil for 5 minutes on each side. Cool. Cut avocado in half and remove skin and seed. Cut avocado into chunky pieces. Sprinkle liberally with lemon juice. Lace shrimp, avocado and scallops alternately on skewers. Mix mayonnaise and vodka together. Spoon into a small bowl. Serve on a circular plate with the sauce for dipping in the center.

Shrimp and Pineapple

Indulge your guests with this enticing cuisine. The decorative pineapple, a symbol of hospitality, adds color as well as appetite appeal.

1 oz. Grand Marnier
1 cup thousand island dressing
1/2 fresh pineapple
1 lb. cooked shrimp

Combine the Grand Marnier with dressing. Cut fresh pineapple in half and cut out pineapple chunks with a grapefruit knife. Fill scooped out pineapple with cubed pineapple pieces and shrimp. Pour sauce over the fruit and shrimp. Place pineapple on platter and serve with toothpicks. Serves 4 to 6 guests.

Crabmeat Dip

This dip is perfect for a cocktail party, or a pleasure before dinner or a luncheon. Chunks of crabmeat adhere to Triscuits or Triangles. (Chips are possible, but I find the dip a little too heavy for them.) This combination disappears fast. I frequently double the recipe in hopes of tasty leftovers the next day!

**1 pkg. (8 ozs.) cream cheese
1 pkg. (6 ozs.) frozen crabmeat
1 tbs. instant minced onion
1/4 cup mayonnaise
2 tbs. seafood cocktail sauce
1/4 tsp. prepared horseradish**

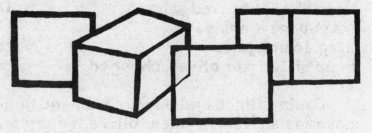

Defrost crabmeat and remove any cartilage. Let cream cheese soften at room temperature. Mix all ingredients early in the day as the flavor is enhanced after remaining in the refrigerator. Serves 6 to 8 guests.

Salmon-Stuffed Cherry Tomatoes

This attractive combination adds variety as well as zest to your hors d'oeuvre platter. If you grow your own cherry tomatoes and are wondering what to do with an over-abundant crop, think appetizers, and capitalize on diversity from your garden.

1 can (7-1/2 ozs.) red salmon
1/3 cup mayonnaise
1 tsp. lemon juice
1 cup pitted ripe olives, chopped

1/2 stalk celery, diced
1/2 tsp. prepared horseradish
cherry tomatoes
chives, chopped

Drain salmon and remove skin and bones. Flake salmon and blend with mayonnaise, lemon juice, olives, celery and horseradish. Slice tops from cherry tomatoes with a grapefruit knife. Remove pulp (which can be frozen and saved for future spaghetti sauce). Stuff salmon mixture into tomatoes and sprinkle with chives.

Lox and Cream Cheese Rolls

Lox and cream cheese have enjoyed a long, happy relationship. Add this delicacy to your hors d'oeuvre platter for an appealing taste treat.

3/4 lb. lox (smoked salmon)
2 tbs. chopped onion
1 pkg. (8 ozs.) cream cheese
2 tbs. cream

Cut each slice of salmon (lox) into 2 inch lengths. Whip cream cheese, cream and onion. Spread each piece thinly but completely with cheese mixture. Roll into shape of a log. Arrange on plate with seam side down. You may want to accompany with crackers. Makes about 18 appetizers.

cold | Hors D'Oeuvres Cheese

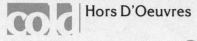
Garlic-Herbed Cheese

Today there are a variety of spreads available with garlic and herbs. This tastes very much like the popular Boursin, but costs a great deal less. It freezes well so you can make it ahead of time to have on hand for unexpected company. Serve with Bremner Wafers.

1 cup, plus 2 tbs. unsalted butter
1-1/2 tsp. parslied garlic salt
3/4 lb. bulk cream cheese
or 1-1/2 pkgs. (8 ozs. ea.) cream cheese
1/2 tsp. dried parsley
1/2 tsp. freeze-dried chives

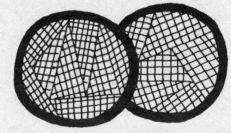

Melt butter in pan and add garlic salt. Simmer 5 minutes, stirring to blend salt. Refrigerate to harden. Whip hardened butter with remaining ingredients, using an electric mixer to blend well. Divide mixture into two crocks or ramekins, or shape into two balls. Refrigerate overnight allowing flavors to blend. This keeps well in refrigerator for several days.

Cheese Ball

Cheese balls come in all varieties. This is a delicious, mild, yet flavorful recipe. Make plenty, and you'll be glad because everyone will enjoy it.

1 container (8 ozs.) sharp cheddar
   cold pack cheese
3/4 lb. bulk cream cheese
or 1-1/2 pkgs. (8 ozs. ea.) cream cheese
2 tbs. chopped chives

1 tsp. dehydrated, minced onion
1 dash Tabasco
1 tsp. Worchestershire sauce
2 tbs. Madeira wine

Bring both kinds of cheese to room temperature. Whip together with an electric mixer. Add chives, dehydrated onion, Tabasco, Worchestershire sauce and Madeira. Line a bowl with clear plastic wrap. Pack cheese mixture into the bowl and use excess wrap to cover. Refrigerate 2 to 3 hours. Turn upside down onto a plate and remove plastic wrap. Serve with a selection of crackers. Cheese ball will keep in refrigerator for several days and freezes well.

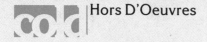
Cheese Spread

This is a mild spread that everyone will enjoy. Prepare a day or two before serving to enhance the flavor

1/4 lb. bulk cream cheese
or 1/2 pkg. (8 ozs.) cream cheese
1-1/2 lb. sharp cheddar cold pack cheese
1 tsp. prepared horseradish
1 tsp. Worcestershire sauce
2 ozs. Madeira

Using an electric mixer whip cream cheese until soft and creamy. Add cheddar cheese in small amounts until combined. Add horseradish, Worcestershire sauce and Madeira. Continue to blend until mixture is smooth and creamy. Fill crockery jar or ramekin with mixture. Serve with crackers.

Distinctive Cheeses

Many varieties of cheese are a familiar sight on today's cocktail table. They are delicious, convenient and deserve recognition. Consult your local cheese store for the unusual as well as for help in selecting the best combinations. Arrange the cheese on a board or platter surrounded by small bunches of grapes for color. Serve with mild crackers such as Bremner Wafers, Carr's Table Wafer Biscuits and Stoned Wheat Thins, which can be found in supermarkets in the gourmet foods section.

A few of my favorite cocktail cheeses are:

Cheddar with Port Wine — A sharp-tasting spread.

Boursin — A creamy cheese with garlic and herbs.

Alouette — A creamy cheese spread with herbs and spices.

Brie — A soft, ripened cheese, cut in wedges. The top and bottom have a moldy appearance. Leave as is and cut pieces from the wedge with a knife.

Muenster — A soft, pungent cheese. Serve in thin slices.

Jack Cheese — Creamy in color with a delicious flavor. Serve in thin slices.

Havarti — A soft, mild Danish cheese.

cold | Hors D'Oeuvres Vegetable

Marinated Mushrooms

Anticipate that there will be no trace left when you offer these savory mushrooms as your hors d'oeuvre selection. They are delicious!

1-1/2 lbs. fresh mushrooms
1 cup bottled Wishbone Italian Dressing
1/4 cup red wine vinegar
1 onion, sliced
1/2 tsp. sugar
1 shallot clove, finely chopped
1/4 to 1/2 tsp. oregano
1/2 tsp. garlic salt

Wash mushrooms and cut into thick slices. Steam for one minute. Combine other ingredients in a glass or ceramic bowl. Add mushroom slices and marinate for at least 3 days in the refrigerator. Mushrooms will keep for weeks if desired.

Marinated Mushrooms and Artichokes

This combination is an engaging one. Two favorites in one dish! Such little effort for such pleasant cocktail fare.

3/4 cup water
6 tbs. tarragon vinegar
2 tbs. white wine
1/4 cup salad oil
1 clove garlic, finely chopped
1/2 tsp. salt

1/4 tsp. pepper
1/2 tsp. thyme
1/4 tsp. oregano
1/2 tsp. tarragon
1 pkg. frozen artichoke hearts
3/4 lb. fresh mushrooms

Combine water, tarragon vinegar, wine, salad oil, garlic, salt, pepper, thyme, oregano and tarragon to make marinade. Cook artichoke hearts as label directs until tender. Drain. Slice mushrooms and steam for 1 minute. Combine artichokes, mushrooms and marinade. Marinate for several days in refrigerator. Serve in dish with hors d'oeuvre picks or cocktail forks.

Guacamole

Guacamole is a versatile spread or dip that has become a very popular addition to the American cocktail table. This is a marvelous version. Serve with Nacho Cheese or Taco Flavor Tortilla Chips.

1 large ripe avocado

1/4 tsp. garlic salt

1-1/2 tbs. lime juice

2 tbs. margarine

1 tsp. finely chopped canned chili pepper

1-1/2 tsp. chili pepper juice

1 tbs. grated onion

1/2 medium tomato, chopped

1 tbs. mayonnaise

Mash avocado well with fork. Melt margarine and add to avocado. Stir in remaining ingredients and blend well. Place the avocado pit in the mixture until ready to serve to prevent the guacamole from turning dark. Cover with plastic wrap.

INDEX TO HORS D'OEUVRES SECTION

METRIC CONVERSION CHART

**Liquid or Dry Measuring
Cup (based on an 8 ounce cup)**

1/4 cup = 60 ml
1/3 cup = 80 ml
1/2 cup = 125 ml
3/4 cup = 190 ml
1 cup = 250 ml
2 cups = 500 ml

**Liquid or Dry Measuring
Cup (based on a 10 ounce cup)**

1/4 cup = 80 ml
1/3 cup = 100 ml
1/2 cup = 150 ml
3/4 cup = 230 ml
1 cup = 300 ml
2 cups = 600 ml

**Liquid or Dry
Teaspoon and Tablespoon**

1/4 tsp. = 1.5 ml
1/2 tsp. = 3 ml
1 tsp. = 5 ml
3 tsp. = 1 tbs. = 15 ml

Temperatures

°F		°C
200	=	100
250	=	120
275	=	140
300	=	150
325	=	160
350	=	180
375	=	190
400	=	200
425	=	220
450	=	230
475	=	240
500	=	260
550	=	280

Pan Sizes (1 inch = 25 mm)

8-inch pan (round or square) = 200 mm x 200 mm
9-inch pan (round or square) = 225 mm x 225 mm
9 x 5 x 3-inch loaf pan = 225 mm x 125 mm x 75 mm
1/4 inch thickness = 5 mm
1/8 inch thickness = 2.5 mm

Pressure Cooker

100 Kpa = 15 pounds per square inch
70 Kpa = 10 pounds per square inch
35 Kpa = 5 pounds per square inch

Mass

1 ounce = 30 g
4 ounces = 1/4 pound = 125 g
8 ounces = 1/2 pound = 250 g
16 ounces = 1 pound = 500 g
2 pounds = 1 kg

Key   (America uses an 8 ounce cup - Britain uses a 10 ounce cup)

ml = milliliter
l = liter
g = gram
K = Kilo (one thousand)
mm = millimeter
m = milli (a thousandth)
°F = degrees Fahrenheit

°C = degrees Celsius
tsp. = teaspoon
tbs. = tablespoon
Kpa = (pounds pressure per square inch)
This configuration is used for pressure
cookers only.

Metric equivalents are rounded to conform to existing metric measuring utensils.